NOW YOU KNOW

D1385151

 # What People Are Saying about *Now You Know*

Over the past decade, Ryan has trained some of the top salespeople in the United States by teaching them the information in this book. Now You Know is designed to take your sales strategy—or your team—to the next level.

TONY JEARY
"The RESULTS Guy" and Coach to the World's Top CEOs
www.TonyJeary.com

Now You Know is a rare book that teaches people how to positively connect in a way that no previous sales technique book has.

GARY SMALLEY
Best Selling Author and Speaker

For years, Ryan Chamberlin has been inspiring and educating people from stage. Finally, he has taken his gift of teaching and put his ideas and proven techniques on paper.

CHRIS WIDENER
Best-Selling Author of *The Angel Inside, The Art of Influence*, and *The Leadership Rules*
www.ChrisWidener.com

Without question, this is the best sales book I have ever read. I have applied the techniques Ryan teaches in this book in various areas of my professional life and they work like magic.

FRANK VISCUSO
Co-author of *The Mentor* and author of *Step Up and Lead!*
www.frankviscuso.com

"Why couldn't I have found this book when I first started in the Industry" is the most common remark I hear from people who read Now You Know. *Ryan's delivery is Spot-On!*

ERIC GOLDEN
Speaker & Author of *The DNA of Business*
www.goldenstandardseminars.com

Every time I turn around in the industry of direct sales I hear about Now You Know *as a trusted resource. After reading it, <u>now I know</u> why.*

VINCE POSCENTE
CEO of the Big Goals Fast Institute
New York Times* Bestselling Author of *The Age of Speed

2ND EDITION

Forward by TONY JEARY America's Coach to the Worlds Top CEO's

Ryan CHAMBERLIN

NOW YOU KNOW

Why some succeed and others fail using the same system

PUBLISHED BY NOW YOU KNOW PRESS IN ASSOCIATION
WITH CARPENTER'S SON PUBLISHING

Published by
Now You Know Press
12305 SE 55th Ave Road
Belleview, Florida 34420

in association with
Carpenter's Son Publishing
Franklin, Tennessee

Cover design: Debbie Sheppard/www.manninggroupdesign.com
Cover photos: Christine Kozlik/www.dovephotos.com
Interior design: Erica Jennings/www.jenningsdesignonline.com
ISBN-13: 978-0-9830914-0-0 (paperback)
ISBN-13: 978-0-9830914-1-7 (hardcover)

Printed in the United States of America.

10 9 8 7 6 5 4 3

This book is dedicated to my wife and four boys.

It is also dedicated to all those living their life in the pursuit of excellence.

 # CONTENTS

FOREWORD

Are you performing at the highest levels in your personal and professional life? If not, what's holding you back? Is it possible you have a blind spot? If you're not where you want to be, you need to read this incredible book. I met Ryan Chamberlin after he read my book *Life is a Series of Presentations*. Although he was already highly successful, Ryan is the type of leader who is always looking to take his game to the next level, and so he asked me to coach him. I realized from the moment we met that Ryan was an exceptional leader in the area of sales and marketing. He also has a gift for inspiring people. He's been speaking and coaching others for years, inspiring them to the next level and leading by example.

After Ryan sent me his audio entitled "The 7 Laws of the System" (on which this book is based), I knew he had a message that needed to be shared with sales professionals across the globe. These seven laws have been practiced and perfected so well that anyone who doesn't read this book is doing himself or herself a great disservice.

As a public speaker, Ryan has a unique energy that he brings to his talks, and he is a great motivator who has the ability to lead teams and individuals to success. I write a lot about clarity, focus, and execution. Ryan has the ability to focus people in a way that brings clarity to their business process. He inspires them to take action today, and he brings a fresh approach to sales, recruiting, and team building. Getting to the root of perfecting the sales process and inspiring people to take action are among his greatest strengths.

You might be succeeding now, but not at the rate you would like to be. Alternatively, you might want to reach that next level, but you find yourself or your team struggling, unable to figure out what the missing piece of the puzzle is. This book can help you. The seven laws taught in *Now You Know* can absolutely transform your business.

Now You Know is not about sales pitches. It is about learning how to influence people in a way that can earn you millions. *Now You Know* is also not about tactics. It is about principles that, when applied within any sales system, allow you to go from the average salesperson to a top 5 percent influential sales master.

Over the past decade, Ryan has trained some of the top salespeople in the United States by teaching them the information he has finally compiled in this book. *Now You Know* is designed to take your sales strategy—or your team—to the next level.

Tony Jeary, "The RESULTS Guy"
Coach to the World's Top CEOs

 # ACKNOWLEDGMENTS

THERE ARE MANY people responsible for the completion of this book—so many that it would be impossible for me to mention everyone. Thank you all from the bottom of my heart.

To my four boys, Alexander, Andrew, Anthony, and Avery, I love you very much. Thank you for your patience while your dad worked on this book.

Most of all, thank you to my beautiful wife, Jenny. You have been through it all with me. You are my partner, and my best friend. I love you.

NOW YOU KNOW

Why some succeed and others fail using the same system.

THERE ARE distinctions that separate you from the highest income earners in your industry? How is it that some sales organizations always outperform others? What is it that could give you the edge in your market to always be at the top? What if these answers are so simple—they're hard?

When most people think of sales, they think of a slick-talking, quick-witted person who, as they say, "could sell ice to an Eskimo." These comments generally make me laugh because not one of the hundreds of top-producing salespeople I've worked with resembles this character. When I was younger, I often wondered how society had come up with such an incorrect perception of what true sales is. All I can think is that a few good salespeople are overrun by thousands of bad ones. In fact, the really good ones are so rare, they are hard to find. They might only account for 5 percent of all sales professionals, which means that for every 1000 salespeople, 950 are breaking one or more of the seven laws you will be exposed to in this book.

I was guilty of breaking these laws. I was twenty years old when I began my career in sales. I was introverted and reluctant to try to take control of a conversation. I failed miserably in sales early on because I didn't know what I didn't know; however, while still in my twenties, I eventually figured it out and earned my first million. I have since developed the sustainable success in sales that has allowed my family the ability to enjoy an incredible lifestyle that most people only dream of.

At one time, the thought of huge success seemed highly improbable to me. Just a few years prior to the understanding of these seven laws, I was working a high-tech job as a packaging technician. This was the title I used to mask the official title of bag boy. I even manufactured my own name badge with this new title clearly printed on it. It seemed to gather customer laughs, and at the same time, it gave me something to talk to them about. I later was honored with the best-bagger award and was sent to (get ready for this) the Bagger Olympics. This was where the top baggers from 100 stores throughout the state were sent to compete. I can still hear the "Chariots of Fire" music playing in the background as I was being graded on speed, grouping of product type, and smile factor with the fake customer. If that doesn't make you laugh, then try to visualize the person grading the baggers—headband, stopwatch, clipboard—as if he stepped out of the movie *Revenge of the Nerds*.

Most people think I'm joking until, in the middle of my public speeches, I display a copy of the certificate that reads as follows:

The status of BEST BAGGER is hereby awarded to Ryan D. Chamberlin for exemplary performance and dedication to customer service, including correct bag usage, well-defined technique, appropriate weight distribution, and superior customer relations. Dated: April 10, 1992.

I know it almost seems like a *Saturday Night Live* skit, but it really happened.

The moral of the story is that if you are struggling, or even if you are succeeding but not at the rate you would like to be, there's hope! And it's here in the form of this book. Even if you are like me and you don't fit the stereotype of the perceived salesperson, you can achieve massive success within your system. *Now You Know* is not about sales pitches. It is about learning how to influence people in a way that can earn you millions. *Now You Know* is also not about tactics. It is about principles that, if applied within any sales system, can allow you to go from the average salesperson to a top 5 percent influential sales master.

Now You Know

To sustain a successful career in sales, you must continually develop both your character and your skills. These two are inseparable.

Over the past decade, I have been fortunate enough to work with and train some of the top salespeople in the United States. While still in my early twenties and under the mentorship of several professionals, I started to become aware of the laws that are revealed in this book.

Once I began applying these laws within my system, I accelerated my career, becoming one of the top producers within my company. After several years of sustained growth, I moved into additional leadership roles, including heading up training divisions, serving on boards, and co-pioneering several sales systems. These systems currently help produce hundreds of millions of dollars in revenue every year. In more recent years, I have spent the majority of my time consulting and coaching many top salespeople on how to leverage themselves, maximize their team-building efforts, and continue to grow to the next level. Most of these top producers are no more intelligent than the average person in their companies, and most do not come from years of previous sales training.

In addition to the many top salespeople with whom I have worked, I have also spent time with hundreds of "could be" top producers. In fact, if you are reading this book and are not a top producer in your company, you are a "could be" top producer. What is the difference between the "could be" top producer, and the top producer? They all have access to the same systems. They all are taught the same steps. Years of reflecting on these questions has led me to the following answer: To sustain a successful career in sales, you must continually develop both your character and your skills. These two are inseparable.

Early in my career, I had two major experiences that directed me down the path of sustainable sales. The first was at the age of twenty, when a friend handed me a box with about fifty cassette tapes and encouraged me to listen to them. I had never listened to tapes before, but I began the process. These audios were from some of the most successful minds of our time.

The sales skills and principles taught on those tapes transformed my thinking. It only took me a few weeks to listen to all of them. I was hooked on self-education and personal growth. I developed an appetite to absorb the best possible information I could on the subject. I also noticed that listening to these tapes had a major impact upon my attitude. Looking back, this was one of the most pivotal points in my career. This habit continues to this day.

Now You Know
The best opportunities in America are presented to those with the leadership ability to handle them. How strong is your leadership ability?

The second experience occurred when I was twenty-two, and the pastor of the church I attend in Belleview, Florida, administrated a leadership series by Dr. John Maxwell. Through this video program, I began to understand why it was important that I develop leadership qualities. I started to understand that the best opportunities in America were presented to those with the leadership ability to handle them. For this reason, it is no wonder that those wishing to be respected as being at the top of their fields pursue character and leadership development.

This book assumes that those of you reading it already possess the character required to succeed. It is written precisely for those who are attempting to follow their companies' systems, but are not seeing the results they feel they should. Is essence, if you are doing everything you are being told and are still not getting results, it's because you don't know what you don't know. That's about to end! *Now You Know* will clarify seven laws of your sales system that are commonly broken, and in most cases, not even thought about.

In addition, I will also reveal a skill set that has helped hundreds of salespeople go from average to above average in a very short time. I will prove that the application of these principles will cause any simple system to do what it has been designed to do in the first place—take you to the top of your game.

Finally, within every successful company, there is a sales team that has perfected a system. These systems contain the mechanics for sales success. The top leaders in your industry have proven this. *Now You Know* will reveal why your system may—or may not—be working for you. It will give you the right tools to transform your business life.

CHAPTER ONE

LAW I:
THE LAW OF THE FIRST IMPRESSION

People do business with people they know, like, and trust.

First impressions matter. There's no doubt that you've heard it at least once in your lifetime, but it's true, isn't it? We are visual beings with five senses, and we use all of them to make quick judgments about the people we meet. When you first encounter new people, your eyes scan their clothing and facial features. Their body language tells a story. Your ears absorb their dialect, and without even being conscious of it, you examine their words, their accents, and their motives. Your brain works like a computer processor to analyze the information within the first few minutes. Your initial impression is a kaleidoscope of previous impressions—a merger of life experiences, judgments, and belief systems. First impressions are powerful, and in sales, the first impression you make is vital to your success.

I didn't always make a good first impression. In the mid '90s, I was not what you would consider a high roller. I drove an '89 Honda Accord. It had four working doors and three working windows. It was so loud that you could hear me coming from miles away. If it wasn't the constant high-pitched squeal of incorrectly installed brake pads, it was the sonic clicking of the busted CV joints that rattled with every turn of the faded steering wheel. Every hundred miles or so, I had to fill the oil and check the gas. Did I mention it had three working windows? Of course it was the driver's door window that would not roll down. This was okay until those times when I decided to visit our local McDonald's drive-through. As if it wasn't bad enough that I had to order my food by opening my door, where we live, the McDonald's has concrete curbs, for safety, by the pick-up windows. The curbs were designed to keep people from being able to open their car doors. I'll never forget the first impression I made with the drive-through assistant when I pulled up in this car. My wife, embarrassed from about what was to happen, simply turned her head in the opposite direction. I had learned to pull my vehicle past the window about three feet, roll down the back left window, lift the recline lever on my seat, lean all the way back, and, in a fully horizontal position, have the assistant hand me my food. Now that I look back, I realize that the weird look on the employee's face at the drive-through was my first impression going down the drain. It's certainly humorous to think about now, but not so much when it was happening. This was one of my first major lessons with the Law of the First Impression.

The Law of the First Impression is not only the starting point of any sale; it is also the most important law to master. This is where the stage is set for the rest of any sales process. Making a great first impression often determines your success in any sales scenario, yet it is violated more than anyone would like to admit. The first impression begins within thirty seconds of making an acquaintance, and it pertains to how you interact with someone prior to selling your product.

LAW #1, THE LAW OF THE FIRST IMPRESSION, STATES, "PEOPLE DO BUSINESS WITH PEOPLE THEY KNOW, LIKE, AND TRUST."

Know, Like, and Trust

The principle of the first impression can be summed up with one straightforward sentence: "People will do business with and refer business to people they know, like, and trust." In his book *Endless Referrals: Network Your Everyday Contacts into Sales,* author Bob Burg shows how business owners and sales professionals can shift their networking from an "activity" that they "go do" a few times a week to a way of life that becomes a part of "who they are" rather than just "what they do." Burg's book helped me understand that the key to sales is building and leveraging your relationships.

Now You Know
People begin to decide whether to purchase your product or service before you ever start to sell it. The close begins in the first thirty seconds.

Often, salespeople begin the sales process too soon. They are so anxious to make the sale that they fail to connect on an emotional level with their prospects. In the fast-growing industry of direct sales, for example, you are trying to gain a business partner and sell your product. If you've only met someone a few minutes ago and you try to sell him on the fact that he should get on autoship with your product, or be in business with you before he knows, likes, and trusts you, you will encounter a great deal of resistance, not to mention a high percentage of negative reactions—and rightfully so. If, instead, you take the time to cultivate the relationship (which may not take much time at all), that same person could end up becoming a valuable asset, either as a customer, for referrals, or a as a business associate. The reality is that people begin to decide whether to purchase your product or service before you ever start to sell it. Many salespeople fail to understand that the close begins in the first thirty seconds. The know, like, and trust principle applies to any sales scenario, regardless of your product or service. This factor refers to your people skills.

People skills are powerful. They represent both the character side and the skill side of your life. Everything you will learn in this book is affected by your level of people skills. Nothing sets the tone for your first impression better than how you deal with people. In Dale Carnegie's book *How to Win Friends and Influence People,* he offers some very practical ways to develop the know, like, and trust factor you need to succeed in sales. Carnegie says, "Become genuinely interested in other people." He emphasizes that smiling is paramount to the first impression. A big strategy he offers is this: "Remember that a man's name is to him the sweetest and most important sound in any language." (Unfortunately, some salespeople overdo this one and insist on repeating a name over and over.) Carnegie teaches us to become good listeners and to encourage others to talk about themselves. Finally, he says, "To make people like you instantly, simply learn to get the other person to feel important—and do it sincerely." The bottom line is that good people skills are a required part of an effective first impression. These skills are important enough to continue developing them during your entire career because they will not only play a key role in helping you to get people to know, like and trust you, they will also enhance all other areas of your life.

Throughout the years, I have had the privilege of spending time with many top money earners in the sales industry. They worked with various companies that offered different products and services. No two had the same personality, and each used his or her own company's proven sales system (and yes, every company has a sales system). These top money earners' techniques and mannerisms were different, but they all had one very big thing in common: within a matter of minutes, people felt like they *knew* them. They had a knack for making people feel valuable and important to the point where people had to *like* them. In addition, because of the way they conducted themselves, a natural relationship began to develop very quickly. This led to *trust*. What amazed me is that they did this without ever mentioning their product. Their people skills were impeccable, and they made a great first impression. They knew that the most important thing most people want to talk about is themselves, and they expressed sincere interest in listening to others do just that. Simply put, when you leave the presence of someone like this, you immediately begin to look forward to the next time you will have the opportunity to be around him or her again.

Now You Know

Top money earners all have one very big thing in common: within a matter of minutes, people feel like they know them.

In contrast, I have also spent a great deal of time around knowledgeable salespeople who have poor people skills. These individuals know their products inside and out, forward and backward. Some even train others on all the best ways to sell the product or service. The interesting issue with many of the individuals that I'm writing about is their lack of actual sales. They are great at acting as if they know everything, but they never seem to get anywhere with their own prospects. A big mistake many of them make is that, within minutes after meeting a prospect, they are already trying to sell their product without taking time to establish a relationship. In many cases, these salespeople never even took the time to learn the prospect's first name. The best analogy for this process is that it's like jumping straight into marriage without going out on a first date. The prospects don't even begin to feel like they know the salesperson.

In addition, when the prospect doesn't react the way these knowledge-able salespeople want, they try to sell harder. This leads to natural reactions of dislike. These people often hear the client's words, "I'm not interested," or "I'm really busy right now," as a polite put-off by their turned-off prospect, but unfortunately, the salesperson would actually think the prospect was interested. This ends up in a negative, snow-balling effect. When the salesperson does finally get approval to call the prospect, the prospect avoids him because of the lack of trust. When this type of salesperson sets appointments, he never seems to close the deals.

You may ask, "If they know their product inside and out, why can't they sell it?" The answer is that these individuals make a BAD first impression. In sales, you create a BAD first impression when you speak or act in such a way that keeps your prospect from getting to know, like, and trust you. In many cases, this could be the only thing a person wanting to be highly successful in sales lacks. What if you make a bad impression and never know it? What if you've made bad impressions in the past, but your clients were too polite, apathetic, or busy to let you know? There are many people out there who fail time and time again because they are not self-aware. They have no idea what kind of impression they're making on others. Think about this, your relationships with people are not solely based on how you feel about them. They are equally based on how people feel about you.

I don't want you to think there is a ton of psychology that needs to be learned before you can begin to achieve success with your system. As a matter of fact, this book offers the opposite alternative. The reality is that sales can be so simple—it's hard. You actually need to learn less than what you are conditioned to think you must know. One of the biggest mistakes most people make is that they tend to overthink the process. The first impression should be understood as the point at which people decide whether they will begin—or continue—to accept the information the salesperson is delivering. Generally, when people feel like they know you and relate to the point that they like you, trust begins to build. This is the point at which, as salespeople, we should begin the process of selling. Any time prior to this point is often disastrous.

Once the process of know, like, and trust is mastered, you need to realize that there can be innocent words you may be using incorrectly. These words can send subliminal signals to your prospect, creating unnecessary skepticism. Most of the time, these are accidental words that are often used before the sales process even begins. These words end up sabotaging your efforts, and they send the average salesperson spiraling down the never-ending path of self-destruction. These words are known as first impression killers, and although they may differ slightly depending on your product or goal, they have an incredible impact on your success.

First Impression Killers

What are the first impression killers of your business? This question is important for you to answer if you want to maximize your system. Of course, a person can dress or act in a way that is unprofessional, but the first impression killers I want to make you aware of in this section are the ones that happen when you are speaking with a prospect. They are the accidental words that you or your sales team may be using that initiate a poor first impression. Yes, they are innocent words. In fact, most people don't even realize what they are saying and therefore can't avoid these words. These are words that violate the value of the know, like, and trust principle. As Dr. Phil McGraw says, "You can't change what you won't acknowledge." It's now time to acknowledge a few things. We can start out by stating that when people get nervous, they begin saying things they shouldn't. These words often lead to many different types of first impression killers. Often, people are nervous about the potential outcome of a conversation, and they are unsure of the potential questions their prospect may ask. This can easily lead to the insecurities that create the wrong first impressions. Now that you will consciously begin thinking about this law while you move through the process of your sales system, you will begin to develop a sense of security. From this moment on, you will understand what the professionals of your company have already mastered, and begin to enjoy their results.

The principles in the following three examples will work in any sales industry. Regardless of whether you sell real estate, automobiles, or advertising space, you can benefit from these examples as long as you relate them to your specific company or product. Here are the top 4 first impression killers in the direct sales industry: the words "business opportunity," "meeting," "got involved with," and "best." The point here is to notice how simple wrong words can kill a first impression.

Example #1: "Business Opportunity"

Let's say you are calling Bob with the intention of inviting him to look at your business. Bob is a warm contact. He's someone whom you've known for a while and someone you think would want to hear about the opportunity you have your hands on. You already have a know, like, and trust relationship with Bob. A common call, complete with a subconscious first impression killer, could go like this:

"Bob, this is Ryan Chamberlin, how's everything going?"

"Great!" replies Bob.

"Listen, Bob, I've got a business opportunity to run by you."

Although this statement seems innocent enough to the novice, it's actually an extreme violation of Law #1. Here's the problem with the words "business opportunity." The caller simply did not think through what Bob's reaction might be when he heard these simple words. Put yourself in Bob's shoes for a moment. I'll bet that, over the years, Bob has heard the term "business opportunity" so much that it sends an instantaneous message to his brain that cause an automatic defensive mechanism to kick in. The funny thing is that Bob doesn't even know why he reacts this way. Maybe he doesn't mean to, but he immediately begins to shut down the notion that you have something worth listening to because of the negative situations that have accompanied these two words in his past. Whether it be infomercials that turned him off, overly aggressive family members trying to sell the latest deal they're into, or the fact that Bob himself has tried four or five other business opportunities—you simply don't want to compete with this. So don't!

One little twist on that phrase can make all the difference. Instead of using the words "business opportunity," what if you said something like this?

"Bob, this is Ryan, how's everything going?"

"Fine."

"Do you have a few minutes? I have something I want to run by you. Is now a good time, or should I call you back?"

The simple change to the word something will increase your chances of accomplishing your goal. This will help move Bob through your system so you can build belief and present your business to him. The point is that the words you use are important, and it pays to choose those words carefully.

Example #2: "Meeting"

Consider the negative implication of this lead-in to a question often posed to a prospect:

"Hey, Bob, this is Ryan. Listen, we're having a meeting tonight, and I want to invite you over. Can you make it?"

This phrasing implies that you're trying to get him out of his comfortable home so you can sell him something. Furthermore, when you ask a friend or prospect to come to a meeting with you, he immediately begins to think that if he joins your company, he is going to be expected to attend weekly meetings. Or, he might work in a job that requires him to attend meetings every day. In either case, he will not be excited about the idea of losing another hour or two of his life and being stuck in an uncomfortable chair while listening to a Kevin Trudeau wannabe tell him about the next big thing. That sounds harsh, but that's exactly what your prospect is thinking. If you take the word "meeting" out of your vocabulary and replace it with an alternative phrase, you'll increase your chances of bringing Bob with you.

This simple adjustment creates an entirely different impression:

"Hey, Bob, this is Ryan. Can you swing by at 7:00 tonight? I wanted to get you the details on that project I was talking to you about."

Example #3: "Got Involved With"

The words "got involved with" have an even worse effect on people. Think about ways you have heard those words used together in the past: "Mary got involved with those kids that were expelled from school." "Billy got involved with that guy who was selling XYZ." Don't forget, it wasn't too long ago that hundreds of people "got involved with" the Bernie Madoff Ponzi scheme. When you tell a prospect that you just got involved with something, his immediate thoughts go to something negative, which again violates the Law of the First Impression.

If you're talking with your prospect and you say, "Hey, listen Bob, I got involved with a company called XYZ," you are implying that you want Bob to get involved with something as well. Immediately, your prospect's mind will start to shut down to the opportunity because he's thinking, "Okay, what is this person trying to get me involved with?"

Make a minor adjustment, and you could change the outcome of this scenario entirely.

"Hey, Bob, this is Ryan. Jenny and I have run across something we want to get your opinion on. Is now a good time, or should I call back?"

The last example I'll give generally applies to product based companies, and it involves the misuse of the word "Best."

"Hey Johnny, I've found this xyz product that's the BEST on the market."

Now before Johnny even starts to listen, questions start rolling through his mind like "Yeah right, if this is the best product out there, how come I've never heard of it?" or "What are you trying to sell me now?"

This type of thought pattern doesn't happen by accident. It happens because of the words you use. Once you understand this, you can make slight adjustments to prevent your prospects from shutting down before they even try your product.

Instead of proclaiming that your product is superior to every other one on the market, you'd have better results saying something less bold. For example, let's say one of your products is an energy drink or supplement, you can say something like this:

"Bob, I notice you drink a lot of soda. Why don't you try one of these energy drinks? I have been drinking one every day. They are healthy and I definitely feel the difference."

As you can see from these examples, it can be one simple, wrong word that causes your system to fail. Therefore, it could be one simple, minor adjustment that makes all the difference in the world. For this reason, I encourage you to study the proven scripts of your system, listen to your top leaders' training, and take note of the words used by the best. Much of what you need to perfect this part of your system can be learned in a matter of minutes. Also, remember that average salespeople completely overlook the simple things like this. This is why they are average. I know this may seem uncomfortable in the beginning, but with a few tries, you'll master this very quickly.

Social Media and the First Impression

Did you know you could make a lousy first impression on social networks? A while back, I received a call from a doctor who was new to direct sales. He earned a high income and was very established; however, he wasn't diversified in a struggling economy. He chose network marketing as a vehicle to leverage himself. As excited as he was, though, he couldn't seem to produce a sale. Knowing how successful he was, I was intrigued by this, and I agreed to meet with him for a private counseling session.

As we talked, I quickly discovered that he was violating several of these laws. What really caught my attention was when he said that three of his Facebook friends had unfriended him last week. "Back up," I said. "Can you elaborate on that?" He went on to tell me that he was using social networks like Facebook and Twitter to reconnect with old friends and make new ones, much like most of the world is doing. However, the moment he made a connection, he would quickly post a comment on that person's wall that resembled a sales pitch from the ShamWow! guy. As a matter of fact, earlier that day he Tweeted and updated his Facebook status to read, "If you are interested in losing weight and making more money, contact me today. You will not want to miss this amazing opportunity."

Now You Know
Keep the conversations centered on the other person, not on yourself; eventually, the subject of your business will come up.

Even though the words he typed were harmless, they came across as desperate. We spoke about the fact that even though these people may have been old acquaintances, he still needed to spend time to get them to know, like, and trust him again. I asked him this question, "If you happened to be walking down the street, and a friend you hadn't seen in more than twenty years ran up to you and said, 'Hi Mike, if you are interested in making more money, call me. You will not want to miss this opportunity,' what would you think?" He admitted that he would have thought the guy had lost his mind and that he would want to run the other direction. I replied, "Well, that's why three of your Facebook friends removed you this week." He got the point.

With the emergence of social media, I strongly encourage you to take advantage of social networks. They allow you to find and reconnect with friends from the past and to connect with other people you would never have the opportunity to meet any other way. Social networks are just one way to develop a powerful first impression and a never-ending referral list. My advice is to use sites like Twitter and Facebook as advertisements into your life. Tweet about and post updates that could be described as lifestyle testimonies. Tell people where you are or where you're going. Have fun and keep it light. When you reconnect with someone new, on Facebook for example, place a comment on his or her wall to initiate dialogue. Ask about this person's family, work, and hobbies; spend time building trust. Keep the conversations centered on the other person, not on yourself; eventually, the subject of your business will come up, and when it does, use your system and follow the advice given in this book.

By the way, if your company has a social network group page, like a Facebook fan page or application, *like it*. Online communities have a language of their own and one of your objectives is to let people know you are part of something in a subtle way. With the right counsel, you can learn how to create enough curiosity that your contacts will begin asking you questions about what you are doing. Joining these groups is a great way to get started.

Posture

If there were ever a concept universal to success in creating first—and lasting—impressions, it would be the concept of posture. Posture works in every area of life. When you were a child, you were told that you needed good posture, but that advice was in reference to how you were sitting or standing. This is a different type of posture. With regard to personal development, and as an overall definition of how posture is discussed in this book, *posture is the way people receive you.*

Posture is ultimately the summation of several character qualities, such as your attitude, belief systems, commitment, and self-image. There are, however, certain principles that, when learned, can have a dramatic effect on how people feel about you and what you say. When you remain in control of the situation and prevent the prospect from gaining control of the sales process, you send subliminal signals of competence, confidence, success, and a multitude of other positive impressions. The challenge with posture is that it cannot be faked. There are three categories of posture that affect your first impression and all other aspects of your system: bad posture, good posture, and true posture.

Bad posture is the result of coming across as needy and/or desperate. Bad posture is the common result when a person gets sucked into letting the prospect control the conversation and dictate who is in charge. This is where 90 percent of all nonproducing salespeople fall and fail. They simply lack the ability to believe in themselves enough to attract the sale. They spend the majority of their short-lived sales careers blaming their lack of success on a system or making some other inaccurate excuse. In reality, it is simply their bad posture that causes a chain reaction of bad responses. When people have bad posture, just like when they break any of these laws, it inadvertently causes a simple system that works well for other people to fail to work for them.

Now You Know
Remember that while good posture is when you *come across like you just don't care*, true posture is getting to the point where *you really don't care.*

Good posture results when you stay in charge of the process. Those with good posture have learned how to deal with a prospect in a confident manner after solidifying a good first impression. They also maintain control when the prospect tries to throw them curveballs. They understand the big picture and display an attitude that tells the prospect that the salesperson does not need any single person to achieve success. Sales professionals with good posture come across to their prospects in a way that says, "I just don't care if you join me or not; either way, this train is moving." You can make a lot of money with good posture.

True posture is what separates the good from the great. While good posture will make you a lot of money, true posture will put you at the top of your game—and at the top of your company. In most cases, there is a natural transition from operating under good posture to eventually moving into true posture. Remember that while good posture is when you *come across like you just don't care*, true posture is getting to the point where *you really don't care*. People have true posture when they have learned to discipline themselves so well on the emotional side of the sales process that the word "no" affects them differently than it affects the average salesperson. In many cases, "no" can even motivate people with true posture. All salespeople who master these seven laws will, over time, develop true posture naturally.

To summarize this chapter, your first impression is largely comprised of your ability to develop a know, like, and trust relationship with your prospect prior to the selling process. It is further enhanced by learning and avoiding the simple first impression killers. And it is maintained and solidified with your level of posture throughout the entire sales process. We will continue to build from these concepts throughout the rest of this book, but if you've been wondering why the initial introduction to your product has been awkward, or why three people unfriended you on Facebook this week, *Now You Know* how the first impression can either make or break any simple system.

CHAPTER 2

LAW II:
THE LAW OF STAYING IN CONTROL

Ninety percent of all sales success begins and ends with staying in control.

Have you ever wondered how a NASCAR driver can stay in control of a vehicle moving at 200 miles per hour through a molasses-thick smoke cloud, while another car is spinning out of control just feet away, and 200,000 fans are screaming at the tops of their lungs? Of course, confidence, experience, and practice come into play, but there is also a simple skill taught to those who learn to drive under these conditions: when you begin to spin out of control, if you fix your eyes on one spot and focus, you will begin to drive toward that spot.

Are you wondering how this applies to sales? In the sales process, there will be many opportunities for your prospect to send you spinning out of control. When you are out of control with your prospect, the posture you are trying to maintain is destroyed. As you uncover the Law of Staying in Control, you will also discover the reasons salespeople lose control. You will learn how to deal with these situations like a pro. Does that excite you? It should, because this chapter could double your income overnight!

While we were still in our first year of marriage, my wife was approached by her coworker at the bank with a unique income opportunity. Jenny began to ask questions of her coworker, who answered them to the best of her ability. Because my wife didn't want to make a decision without speaking with me first, she introduced me to the idea and hoped for my approval. After asking her several pointed questions, I quickly lost interest and dismissed the idea as a waste of time. I squelched any notion of our participating, even though I didn't receive enough information to make an informed and intelligent decision.

Think of the irony of this situation. I was receiving third-party answers to questions that weren't even that important, and I was making an uneducated decision that could affect (and did, in a negative way) the financial future of my family. People do this same thing every day. It wasn't that my wife answered incorrectly, it was that the salesperson had lost control of how and when the information would be delivered. The process was now left up to chance. I was one of the key decision makers, and I had been left out of the process. After all, I was needed to close the deal, and I hadn't even seen the presentation.

In retrospect, I messed up by not getting the facts, and this gave me an easy way out. Several years later, the same financial opportunity came back around, and this time I decided to look at all the information before jumping to a conclusion. It could have been the fact that the person presenting was better at staying in control, or perhaps it was the fact that what I was doing obviously wasn't working, but I was more open-minded about taking a look. Whatever the reason, the fact remains that the more I researched this opportunity, the more appealing it became. This time we participated and had a positive learning experience. Needless to say, I've had egg on my face ever since. My wife somehow reminds me of the fact that she originally brought the same information home, but I, in all my wisdom, turned it down. She was right, and I was wrong. This subject comes up at least once a year, which usually ends with us laughing about the incident. My question to you is this: "How many sales are lost because the salesperson loses control?" I believe the answer is *too many to count*. I am confident that if you master this law, it will be a catalyst for volume and growth within any sales system.

LAW #2, THE LAW OF STAYING IN CONTROL, STATES, "NINETY PERCENT OF ALL SALES SUCCESS BEGINS AND ENDS WITH STAYING IN CONTROL."

Even if a sale doesn't take place, if you remain in control, you will win. Let me explain.

Early on, I had a hard time distinguishing where to draw the line when it came to staying in control. I later found out that this is one of the biggest mistakes made in the sales industry. In my twenties, for example, I would come across potential prospects and initiate a conversation with the goal of creating curiosity about my company. At some point in that conversation, I would tactfully generate enough curiosity that they would begin to ask questions about what I did for a living. I became so confident in my ability to answer any question they threw at me that I welcomed them, maybe even encouraged them, to ask me anything they wanted. Unfortunately for me, I never left a question unanswered. Although I was glad that I had developed the ability to produce answers for my prospects' questions and objections, during this time in my career, I also found it extremely difficult to book *quality* appointments. I didn't have a difficult time initiating conversations, nor did I struggle when it came to generating interest. Why, then, were my prospects not allowing me to set up appointments? What was I doing wrong?

Over time, I became aware that the two key places where I lost control of the sales process were when the prospect started to ask questions and when I was not dealing with all of the decision makers. I also realized that I had an edge on staying in control once I understood that the prospects didn't know what they didn't know. With this in mind, I could literally tell them what they should or should not think about the information they were hearing. I call this *controlled perception*. Let's start with how a salesperson should handle questions.

Dealing with Questions

If you remember that a bad first impression can result in making your sales system ineffective, then you should understand that how you deal with questions—or dealing with questions ineffectively—is where 90 percent of all sales system problems begin after we've started. Thus, Law #2, and dealing with the *how* and *when* to answer questions will account for the majority of staying in control.

Now You Know

If too many questions are asked and answered prior to your presentation, prospects' decisions end up being premature.

You've heard the saying, "Curiosity killed the cat." In sales, it is, "Curiosity gives control." If your prospect is asking questions, it means he or she is curious. Answering these questions at the wrong time, however, eliminates curiosity. When prospects are no longer asking questions, they've generally made a decision about your product. If too many questions are asked and answered prior to your presentation, prospects' decisions end up being premature.

I noticed that the most successful conversations I had were the ones during which my prospects did not ask a lot of questions prior to viewing my presentation. I also became aware that certain personality types were more inclined than others were to ask questions in an attempt to acquire additional information. As these certainties began to materialize in my mind, I concluded that genuine curiosity can only come from *not knowing*. With this conclusion, I was able to develop a style of business and settle on a technique that has helped me rise to the top of the direct sales industry. The concept behind this technique is simple, and I'd like to share it with you right now. Regardless of the questions your prospect asks before booking an appointment to view a presentation, if you develop the skill of properly communicating that the questions are *going to be answered*—instead of presenting too many details—you can maintain and even strengthen the prospect's level of curiosity. Your ability to do this will enhance your posture and result in a higher percentage of qualified appointments.

This law doesn't mean that you should never answer questions or that you should be evasive or rude, as doing that would violate other laws. The law simply introduces the fact that you stay in control of the sales process when you learn to postpone the details that answer most questions until after the presentation. The reality is that your human response is to ask questions before getting all the facts. After all, you are busy. If you can get straight to the point, then you can make a decision more quickly, right?

The answer may surprise you. A faster decision? Yes. An accurate decision? Not quite. It seems contrary to human nature not to answer a simple question, right? Your initial thought might be, "If he's asking questions before the presentation, he must be interested." Most of the time, this is a correct assumption, but by answering his questions, you often eliminate his need to get all the details. The reality is that he may or may not be interested, but what I can guarantee you is that by asking multiple questions, he is trying to develop enough of an opinion to make a decision without having to look at all the facts.

Don't be mad at your prospect for being this way. We live in a society that promises fast results for everything. Most people have an attention span that lasts about as long as the average commercial. They don't want to waste their time, so they try to come to a conclusion without having to look at your product or presentation. When you come to this realization, you will also begin to understand that this is not necessarily a bad thing as long as you also realize that just about any answer you give prior to the complete presentation can come back to haunt you. This holds true even if the question is legitimate.

So what's the answer to this dilemma? You must learn how to deal with questions and harness the power of curiosity throughout the sales process without making the prospect feel like you're avoiding the answer. In any sales system, the best possible results will come when you have a prospect who is genuinely curious during a quality presentation. This is something that cannot happen if you fill your prospect's mind with details before you get to the appointment. Even if you do this and manage to get her to a presentation, she will have been so inundated with unnecessary information that she will miss the simple selling points of your company, product, or compensation plan.

What *is* the answer to every question?

You may be wondering by now how to answer questions when they come up prior to the presentation of your product. Wouldn't it be great if you had the perfect answer for every question? Well, you do! If you master this, you will be able to harness the power of curiosity, and you will experience much greater results that you are getting now.

The answer to every question is . . . the next step in your system. This by far is the most productive way to answer a question. The bottom line is that every question you are asked is a reason to move your prospect into the next step of your system. This is true in any sales industry. If a potential client who is ready to purchase a home asks a real estate agent questions about the prices of homes in a specific area, the agent should take that opportunity to invite the client into his or her office to review some listings. Sending that prospective buyer to a Web site is no different than saying, "Thanks for calling. Check out these listings, and someone else will sell you a home."

In the direct sales industry, it's no different. If my prospect hasn't seen the presentation yet but asks the question, "How much does it cost?" I can answer and have the prospect make a decision without all the facts, or I can say, "That's a great question. We're having a get together at our home tomorrow night to go through the details. Can you swing by about 7:00 p.m? It will be fun. Or, we have a thirty-minute overview [or video, or presentation] that goes through the details. Let's schedule a time when we can go through this and get all your questions answered."

To illustrate further, let us assume you have initiated a conversation about your product or business, and you have begun to move Bob through your system. Your focus is to stay in control of the process. In this example, you have just prequalified Bob by providing some introductory information, perhaps in the form of a link to a short video clip, third-party endorsement, a brief audio, or a prerecorded message.

After the information, Bob says, "What's this all about?" or "How much does this cost?" or "How much money have *you* made?" Realize that if you answer these questions, Bob will begin to formulate his own opinion of what you are doing, and in turn, he will make his decision before the conversation is over. Remember, your goal is to build Bob's curiosity and get him excited about wanting to view all the details. This is where he could hear and/or see another short video clip, success story, or 3rd party phone call to quickly move him toward wanting to view your full presentation. Your system may or may not be different, but the goal is the same.

Let's break down this question that Bob might ask: "How much does this cost?" Know that if you answer this question before running Bob through the sales system, he will begin to think about the cost—and not the value—of what you are offering him. Of course, you don't want to ignore the question. You absolutely must answer it . . . just not at this moment. Instead, you would be better off answering with one of the following statements:

"That's a great question. We're having a get together at our home tomorrow night to go through the details. Can you swing by about 7:00 p.m? It will be fun."

-or-

If you are selling a nutritional product, you may say, "Bob, you and I both know we need to eat better" (or be more health conscious). Can I swing by tomorrow night at 7:00 p.m. so I can give you the details?"

-or-

"Bob, that's a great question. We have a thirty-minute overview [or video, or presentation] that goes through the details. Let's schedule a time when we can go through this and get all your questions answered."

-or-

"Bob, that's a great question. Do me a favor and hang on for a moment so I can get you some more information." This is where you could bring in another team leader for a third-party endorsement."

-or-

"Bob, I know you have a bunch of questions. The next step here is to schedule a time when the two of us can sit down over a cup of coffee and view the details."

—or—

"Bob, obviously this is not enough information to make an intelligent decision. The next step is to set an appointment today or tomorrow for you to view the details. Which is better for you?"

After answering with one of those statements, it's a good idea to try to set a time to get Bob more information, or to set up the appointment with a question like, "What day/night is better for you—Tuesday or Wednesday?"

Remember, your system may have some variations, but I'm sure you understand the point. The top money earners in this industry have discovered that when a prospect starts asking questions, they continue to move the prospect through their system, and ironically, before the process is complete, the prospect usually gets all of his questions answered or forgets the questions altogether once he gets intrigued enough to agree to an appointment.

Dealing with the Decision Makers

Another surefire way to lose control of a sale is to conclude your presentation without the decision makers in the room. What if you're trying to sell a product that will benefit a company, and at the end of your one-hour presentation, you hear this: "This looks great, but I'll need to speak to my manager." Then, after you present to the manager, you hear this: "This looks great, but I'll need to speak to the owner."

How many times have you heard at the end your presentation, "I need to go home and speak to my spouse about this"? The same result will happen 99 percent of the time. You will lose control of the sales process, and you will put yourself at the mercy of an unskilled presenter. Just like in the story at the beginning of this chapter, I might have looked at the presentation the first time if the salesperson at my wife's bank had known what I am about to explain. This scenario had happened to me several times in a row: I had lost control of the sales process and ultimately lost the sale. Finally, I learned the way to head it off and stay in control.

Now You Know

Ask the question, "If you like what you see today, will you be able to make the final decision, or will we need to run it by anyone else?"

First, if you are presenting to a business, then your goal is to present to the owner or the person who has the authority to make the decision. Second, if you are presenting person to person, if possible, book your appointment with both the husband and the wife. Too many sales are lost when this does not take place. If this does not seem possible, then ask this question prior to solidifying your appointment: "If you like what you see today, will you be able to make the final decision, or will we need to run it by anyone else?"

This question gets it all on the table, increases your posture, and eliminates problems during the close. In many cases, the prospect will say something like, "Yes, I would need to show this to my spouse [or the manager, or the owner] prior to making a decision." If this happens, stop right there and set a time when you all can meet. If the prospect says something like, "No, I can make the decision," then you can book the meeting knowing that the prospect will probably not play the spouse card at the closing table. Either way, you're in control.

Controlled Perception

The last concept I will cover in this chapter is what I call controlled perception. This is the proactive approach to staying in control. In most cases, prospects' perceptions are their reality. In many cases, you can dictate what they perceive. Notice that in several of the examples in the "How to Deal with Questions" section, my answers contain a controlled-perception answer. For example, when I answered Bob's question with, "Bob, obviously this is not enough information to make an intelligent decision," I am telling Bob subliminally that it's not okay to say no yet if he is a smart person. Another example of controlled perception is when I said, "Bob, I know you have a bunch of questions. The next step here is to schedule a time when the two of us can sit down and view the presentation." If you notice the verbiage, I am telling the prospect what and how he should be thinking at this point in the process. In most cases, this will strengthen your posture and control the perception the prospect has developed up to that point. You literally are doing the thinking for the prospect. With practice, this can be fun, and in any sales system, you can usually come up with two or three of these statements that you use over and over again.

Now You Know

It's not your presentation alone that makes the sale—it's how someone *feels* about your presentation that makes the sale.

Final Thoughts

You will never stay in control 100 percent of the time, but you absolutely will improve your success ratio by applying Law #2. Staying in control, by default, will result in a higher level of curiosity, a more qualified appointment, and a more positive perception of what you are offering. This means less time wasted on unproductive presentations, which in turn means more sales. The difference between two salespeople's results—when one stays in control and the other doesn't—is not double, it's exponential. Let's face it. If it were your presentation only that sold your product or put people into the business, then all you would have to do is hand out a DVD or send prospects to a Web site. This is simply not the case. Your presentation is only the step that delivers the information so someone can make an intelligent decision about what you are selling. How someone *feels* about the presentation is what makes the sale. If you stay in control while building belief and curiosity, your prospect will be sitting on the edge of his or her seat, curiously watching your presentation. With the Law of Staying in Control, you should constantly ask yourself, "Am I violating this law?"

If you've been wondering why your ratios have been off even though you feel like you understand everything there is to know about your company, and you've been answering every question your prospects have been asking, *Now You Know.*

CHAPTER 3

LAW III:
THE LAW OF
THE TAKEAWAY

People want what they can't have.

Combined with the first impression and the ability to stay in control, the principles in this chapter can create an unstoppable sales machine that causes people to beg you for your product, service, or company.

Have you ever wanted something so badly you could taste it? My teenage son understands the takeaway. When minor discipline is necessary, my wife and I simply take his electronics away for a couple of days, and the message becomes loud and clear. It's amazing to see a young man break out in hives or fall into a depression-like state because we have temporarily taken away his iPod, cell phone, or Xbox.

I will never forget the first time I used the takeaway in sales. It actually happened by accident. Jenny was pregnant with our first child, and I was selling cars for a large used-auto chain in central Florida. A woman and her husband walked onto the lot, and it was my turn to take the prospect. I introduced myself and politely offered to show them the vehicle they seemed to be interested in. Before I knew it, we were on the road, test-driving the vehicle. I was new in the auto sales business and didn't know much about sales in general. I especially struggled with closing the deal. You can imagine my surprise when, out of the blue, the couple told me they would like to purchase the vehicle—"If the price is right." So far, so good, right? After returning to the dealership, I escorted them to my desk and began to fill out the appropriate paperwork to begin the process. After several trips back and forth between the couple and my manager, it looked like I might lose the sale. They definitely wanted the vehicle; however, even though I put my best offer on the table, it seemed that the price was just too high for them. I could see their reluctance, and I felt my heart begin to race when I knew they were ready to walk away from the deal. In one last-ditch effort to get a reaction from the couple, I opened my mouth, and out came these words: "Well, Ma'am, maybe you just can't afford this vehicle." As the words left my mouth, I pulled the contract away from them. The tone I used was wrong. It was somewhat confrontational. I immediately realized this and wished I hadn't said those exact words, but I did get a reaction. First came a piercing look, and then came the woman's frustrated response: "Who are you to tell me what I can and can't afford, young man?"

Now You Know

If it doesn't come naturally for you to follow these laws, you've got to train yourself to do what doesn't feel normal to you in order to succeed.

She looked at her husband and then back at me before saying, "I would like to see the manager." I was instructed later by my manager not to be that harsh with my words, but then he gave me a high-five because I had made the most profitable sale of the day. Although my wording could have been less confrontational, the principle of what happened is what generally happens when you take something away from your prospects—*they want it more.*

You may be thinking that because I am the author of this book, I don't struggle to obey these laws. That is not only inaccurate, it's actually quite the opposite. This law, for example, is contrary to my personality. That does not, however, change the fact that it is absolutely vital that I master this law. It's kind of like the game of golf. To master it, you have to swing and play in a way that feels unnatural. If it doesn't come naturally for you to do something, but you still need to do that one thing to succeed, you've got to go against your natural instinct and train yourself to do what doesn't feel normal to you.

I made the decision early on that I did not want to waste my energy being afraid of something that didn't come naturally for me, especially if that something was going to stand in the way of my family's financial independence. Although the takeaway was something that slightly intimidated me, I fully understood that when someone can't have something, that is when he or she wants it the most. This is the reason the Law of the Takeaway is so important. The reality is that there is no other technique in sales that displays your level of posture better than the takeaway.

LAW #3, THE LAW OF THE TAKEAWAY, STATES, "PEOPLE WANT WHAT THEY CAN'T HAVE."

When we develop true posture, we can remove the emotional connection to the yes or no of the sale. When this happens, the natural reaction when a prospect seeks to gain control of the sales process is simply to *take it away.* In essence, the takeaway is when your prospect takes on any position of hesitancy throughout the sales process, and instead of selling harder, you gain control of that position by taking it away.

Now You Know
Take this philosophy to heart: If you argue with your prospect, even if you are right, you will always lose.

Generally, during the process of selling or recruiting with any product or company, there comes a time when you need to use or reiterate the takeaway to maintain proper posture. It may occur in the first part of your system, before you even begin the prequalification process, or it might pop up right when you're trying to book the appointment. It may be that the prospect begins to argue with something you've said. At this point, a salesperson can get frustrated and may want to spend time convincing the prospect why he or she, the salesperson, is correct. This never works, and it's important to note this philosophy of the professional: if you argue with your prospect, even if you are right, you will always lose.

Throughout the years, I have found that most people understand why the takeaway works—because they have personally experienced it once or twice during their own lives. Think back to your high school days, when you wanted to date someone who clearly wasn't interested in you. As a result, your level of interest in that person grew significantly. It's easy to understand *why* the takeaway works; however, when it comes to sales, what most salespeople confuse is the *when* and *how* to use it.

The following scenarios could be crafted and played out in many different ways. To become a high achiever, you would be wise to begin by accepting the fact that all top producers in this industry use the takeaway on a regular basis. They use it so much that they reach a point at which it becomes second nature to them.

Let's say you're talking to Johnny about your product, or company, and he says, "I don't know if I'm interested."

Instead of wasting your time trying to convince Johnny he should be interested (which is what the average sales professional would do), you could take his position away from him like this:

"Johnny, this may or may not be for you, but wouldn't you agree that it doesn't make sense to make a decision before you look at the details?"

-or-

"Johnny, I'm not even sure if you would benefit from this product the way others have, but we won't know until you give it a try."

-or-

"Johnny, wouldn't you agree that sharp, business-minded people don't try to make decisions before they get all the facts?"

-or-

"Johnny, obviously now is not the right time for you. Do you mind if I call you in sixty days?"

The key here is not to beg Johnny to try your product or see your company, but to take it away by making a key statement that strengthens your posture. This will either shake him into a solid appointment or prevent you from wasting your time.

Amateurs Convince and Professionals Sort

That is really where the takeaway fits into your system. Instead of begging or pleading with your prospects, you are actually creating an atmosphere in which you are in control of whether or not you even want to meet with them in the first place. This is often hard for new salespeople to grasp, simply because they are looking for every opportunity to present their product or company, and they often make the mistake of coming across as if they need their prospects to say yes. It doesn't have to be this way.

If used correctly, the takeaway can even work on answering machines. First, let me explain to you why you won't receive callbacks from certain people. It's because they don't want to call you back! As hard as that is to deal with, it is just a fact. Don't take it personally; just deal with it. Even if you are like me and believe that if people are interested in what you have, they will call you back, it's also essential that you are thorough with following up. To balance this, I recommend a *three-call rule*.

Now You Know

The three-call rule: Assume that if you've left two messages and your calls hasn't been returned, it's time to do the takeaway.

The purpose of this rule is simple: if you continue to leave messages on a prospect's answering machine, over a relatively short period of time, you will ultimately lose the chance to sell him or her your product, service, or company. For this reason, assume that if you've left two messages and your calls haven't been returned, it's time to do the takeaway. If you don't, you will cross the line of selling and venture into begging. This will place you in the category of those with bad posture.

The following example will illustrate what type of message I would leave if the takeaway were needed.

> *"Johnny, I wanted to leave you one final message. If you don't call back, that's okay. I'll just cross you off my list and assume you're not interested."*

If you do this, you must do it with a professional, non-confrontational tone in your voice. You may be wondering, "Why does this kind of message work?" It works because no one wants to be taken off anyone's list. I have used this line—or a variation of it—many times, and I often find myself getting a return call when I could have almost guaranteed I would not have received a call otherwise. Usually, when the prospect calls, it sounds something like this: "Hey, Ryan, don't take me off your list. I'm still interested, but I need a little time because I'm in the middle of a big project at work."

The takeaway may not work 100 percent of the time, but it absolutely increases your odds. The bottom line is that the takeaway works! I also believe that if you handle yourself with the right posture during the entire process, including when you use the takeaway, you will actually gain more respect from your prospect. Coupled with the fact that timing plays a big part of whether or not you make the sale, we can conclude that if you maintain the correct posture with your prospect, there is a strong probability that when the timing is better, you will be the one he or she thinks of when it comes to your area of expertise. Again, proper follow-up and periodic communication become important for this to play out.

Last, the takeaway has certain self-esteem advantages you need to succeed in sales. When you are in a position in which prospects continually tell you that they are not interested, it sends a subliminal message to you, the salesperson, that you are not good enough to share what you have. This translates into your belief system and ultimately reflects in your sales results. However, the opposite occurs when you are the one who is doing the taking away. Every time you decide that it's in your best interest to take it away from a prospect, you are telling yourself that this prospect may or may not deserve your time. This elevates your self-esteem and results in an increasing belief in your ability. This, too, will reflect in your sales results. This time, you will be recognized as a top producer.

Together, the first three laws work synergistically to reinforce your posture. For example, if you master the Law of Staying in Control, you will deal with questions correctly and set the tone of who is in charge. When the time comes that you have to use the takeaway, your prospects will not want you to disqualify them because people will be attracted to you, and people want to follow people they know, like, and trust. *Now You Know* the awesome power of the takeaway!

CHAPTER 4

LAW IV:
THE LAW OF THE BIG ROCKS

Enough qualified appointments will always guarantee your success.

Have you ever wondered why some people are so productive while others are not? Why do some people seem to work less hard or fewer hours than others do—yet they always seem to be way ahead of the pack? The understanding of this simple phenomenon is illustrated by the Law of the Big Rocks.

Let's imagine you are sitting at your desk, and you have a one-gallon bucket in front of you. Also on the desk are four elements: water, sand, pebbles, and large rocks. Imagine that each of those elements represent a different activity required for you to make sales and build a profitable business. The water represents self-education, which includes such things as listening to audios, reading books, and attending company events. The sand represents sending e-mails, returning general phone calls, and making sure everything stays organized. The pebbles represent training and working with new team members to create more volume. The big rocks represent setting qualified appointments through your system. Most new salespeople begin to fill up their buckets with water and sand and pebbles. In other words, they are busy. They are *very* busy attending events, planning strategies, returning phone calls, and training new team members. So busy, in fact, that when it comes time for the big rocks, they realize their bucket is already full, and there is no room—or, more specifically, no time—to do the activity that matters the most, which is *showing the presentation to qualified prospects or customers*. The water, sand, and pebbles are what the majority of people who say they are "busy" are actually doing.

Now You Know

By definition, a qualified appointment is one in which the dominant thoughts of a prospect align with the results that the salesperson is looking for.

How do we solve the problem? We begin by identifying the difference between activity and productivity. You see, all the activities in the examples here are important, but without qualified appointments, you will find them to be senseless and futile. The solution to this dilemma is quite simple: begin to fill your bucket with the more-productive, income-producing activities first. Consider the fact that when you first fill the bucket with water, as soon as you begin to put sand and pebbles in the bucket, the water starts to overflow. Once sand fills the bucket, there is no more room for pebbles, let alone big rocks. Now let's reverse it. If you put the big rocks in first, there will be room for pebbles and sand to fill in the voids. And whatever spaces the pebbles and sand do not fill, the water surely will. To clarify this illustration, if you fill your calendar with qualified appointments, you will find it easy to educate yourself and make calls to your prospects and team members throughout the day, perhaps on the way to those appointments. The results will be more sales and increased income because you are placing an emphasis on the activities that matter the most. The conclusion is this: the big rocks of your business will always be qualified presentations. Without them, you have nothing.

LAW #4, THE LAW OF THE BIG ROCKS, STATES, "ENOUGH QUALIFIED APPOINTMENTS WILL ALWAYS GUARANTEE YOUR SUCCESS."

The Qualified Appointment

Obviously, the big rock illustration sets the stage for how to think productively. And now that we have decided that qualified appointments are the lifeblood of your business, the next step is to get clear about what qualified appointments really are. This is essential, because many people in sales seem to be unaware of the importance of qualified presentations. By definition, a qualified appointment is one in which the dominant thoughts of a prospect align with the results that the salesperson is looking for. Unfortunately, most salespeople are so worried about getting the appointment that they devise crafty verbiage to stay within their comfort zones, often setting a mindset that is light years from the result they want. Although they may successfully book appointments this way, making the sale is now ten times harder because of the incorrect seeds they planted in the prospects' minds. Even if these salespeople do make a sale, the side effects of that sale will surface in the form of the loss of referrals, incorrect duplication, and failure to achieve repeat business. Fortunately, just a little attention in the area of mastering the following principles can have an exponentially positive effect on your career. This understanding and correction begins with what I call a *dominant thought*. To create a dominant thought, though, we must first have leads. Let's begin there.

Lead Generation

As we begin to master the appointment-setting process, it's important to build from the assumption that you have leads. If you do not have leads, then we need to master hot, warm, and cold market-lead generation. There are two primary lead categories.

First Category: Personal Leads

Personal leads include traditional lead sources, such as using a personal memory jogger or browsing the classified section of a phone book to remind yourself of who you know. You can also learn how to use social media Web sites such as Facebook and Twitter. When it comes to generating leads, your options are endless, yet lead generation is one of the biggest excuses people use as to why they don't succeed. Let me just say this and then be done with it—the excuse, "I don't know anybody," is a cover for those who really mean, "The pain of change is greater than the pain of staying the same." My personal viewpoint is that you have met enough people, will meet enough people, or can personally meet enough people to succeed in any sales business—if your desire for success is strong enough. It's not a question of who you know; it's how you apply these laws with the people you contact that will make all the difference. Just remember that the foundation for lead generation is developing a *know*, *like*, and *trust* relationship before you begin to sell.

Second Category: Referrals

This category begins with the understanding of the Rule of 250. If you understand and apply the information in this book, once you begin making sales, you should never run out of leads. The reason for this is simple: during every qualified appointment, you're sitting in front of someone who knows 250 potential prospects they could refer to you. When I finally understood this, my immediate thought was, "Wow! I can't fail as long as I don't stop working."

A good habit to start immediately is to begin asking one very simple question of any quality prospect you come in contact with. The question begins with, "Who do you know that . . ." and ends with something that describes to the result you are looking for. This may seem corny, but I personally have been turned on to great leads from prospects who originally did not purchase my product. These leads, in turn, directed me to substantial contracts that led to millions of dollars. One time, for example, I was sharing both a product and an opportunity with a busy and well-networked contact. Although this business owner was interested in my product, his plate was too full to entertain the opportunity I was explaining. Because I had taken the time to develop a *know*, *like*, and *trust* relationship with him, and because it was obvious that he knew some quality people, I simply made the following statement, "Who do you know that is a sharp business-minded person and would be open to looking at this?" He gave me three names. After communicating with these individuals, one of them ultimately led me to millions of dollars in sales. Not only has this strategy worked for me several times over my career, but I also have witnessed this strategy working for countless others. The bottom line is that you don't get what you don't ask for.

Now You Know
During every qualified appointment, you are sitting in front of someone who knows 250 potential prospects they could refer to you.

The Dominant Thought
Laws #1, #2, and #3 are the foundation for becoming effective in the appointment-setting process, but it's the dominant thought you create that sets the tone of your presentation. The process really begins with defining the dominant thought pattern you want your prospect to be in, which will produce the optimal results for your presentation.

Let's say your primary goal is to build an organization of business partners that then become customers for your direct sales company. You have to understand that any strategy, other than an opportunity-driven one, used to set appointments will most likely end with undesired results.

-or-

Let's say your primary goal is build a large base of satisfied customers that then introduce you to potential distributors. In that instance, your primary focus should revolve around the customer experience and retention. Once a prospect joins your team and/or purchases your product, the dominant thought you created early on will ultimately affect the end result you are looking for. If you try to change your direction midway through the sales process, in most cases, a sale will not take place. Instead, the prospect will feel like you pulled a bait and switch and may resist any involvement with you. You will not only lose the sale, but you will also lose your chance of getting a qualified referral.

Consider these examples:

Example #1
You call John and let him know about the product you have that he needs. You explain that he would be doing you a favor, and he agrees to meet with you. After you present the product, you go right into the marketing plan. John liked the product, but he wasn't expecting to see an opportunity. This turns him off. He tells you he needs time to think about it, and you never seem to be able to get ahold of him again.

Example #2
This time you say something like, "John, I have something I want to run by you. Is now a good time, or should I call you back?" You have John watch a quick video clip on the internet, and ask "What did you like best about what you saw?"

John is interested in business ideas, so his ears perk up. You proceed to let him know that what you've got is 90 percent visual, and you would like to meet him for lunch to go over the details.

-or-

John adds something like, "I certainly would like to get healthy too." You proceed to invite him over tomorrow night to sample the product, and get the details.

Either way, when you meet with John, you are prepared to take him through your system, but more importantly,

John is expecting to go through your system. His attitude is entirely different simply because of the dominant thought you created going into the meeting, and the fact you kept your focus on that dominant thought.

Take the time right now to write down the dominate thought and optimal result for your company, product, or service.

_____

_____

_____

_____

Avoiding Appointment Pitfalls

As good as you become at mastering and implementing the dominant thought, there are a few appointment pitfalls you need to know about. The following four principles will help head off a high percentage of hard-to-book or potentially cancellable appointments.

1. Offer two choices of when to meet.
2. Keep the ball in their court.
3. Present your time as valuable.
4. Be careful of cancellation setups.

Let me explain. When you come to the point in your conversation at which you are ready to set the appointment, offer your prospect two choices of when to meet. A common mistake people make is offering one choice and hearing a response that sounds similar to this: "That day is no good for me. How about I call you next week when I have more time, and we'll try to set it up the appointment then?"

When this occurs, if you try to offer another day of the week, prospects will see you as being desperate. And by waiting until the next week, they will lose interest, and you will find yourself having to build belief again before they agree to set up an appointment.

The best way to avoid this occurrence is to offer two choices right away. The following example shows how you can incorporate the previous statement into this technique.

You say, "John, the next step is to get together and cover some brief information on our program. What day would be best for you—Tuesday morning or Wednesday afternoon?"

John says, "How about Wednesday?"

Although you will set many appointments with this simple approach, obviously they will not all be this easy. It's important to mention that many potentially good appointments are lost when you have an interested prospect but you struggle to figure out what time to meet with him.

Let's say the conversation you just had with your prospect went like this:

You say, "Which would be better, today at 5:00 p.m. or tomorrow at lunch?"

Your prospect replies, "Call me tomorrow and we'll set it up."

Even when a good prospect asks you to call him or her back tomorrow, it usually means, "If you try to call me, I will avoid your call. Even though I like what you are saying, I'm way too busy." It's important that you learn to keep the ball in the prospect's court. By staying noncommittal, the prospect is trying to push the ball into your court so you will have to jump through more hoops to set the appointment. Often, it only takes one simple statement to regain control of the appointment-setting process. Here is an example of what to say after your prospect tries to push off the appointment:

You: "Mr. Smith, I know you're just as busy as I am, so why don't we go ahead and set the appointment for tomorrow, and if something comes up, you can call me to reschedule. What time works better for you—12:00 or 2:00?"

That is just one example of how you can put the ball back in your prospect's court so he has to call back and cancel on you instead of your having to track him down to set up an appointment. The fact is that most people hate to cancel a meeting, so make it your goal at this stage in your system never to get off the phone with a prospect without setting a firm time for both of you to meet. If you put yourself in the mindset that you are going to make every call with specific intent, you will surely set the appointment before getting off the phone. In the scenarios we just described, your specific intent is to set the appointment. Once you do that, you have achieved your goal.

Another scenario you will want to master is avoiding the appearance of not having a full schedule, and instead presenting your time as valuable. People who are good at their jobs are in high demand. Often, when a new salesperson is starting out, he or she reacts to a prospect in this manner:

Prospect says, "I can't meet with you today or tomorrow. Can I call you back?"

New salesperson replies, "Sure thing. I have the entire week open to meet with you; just let me know what works."

Although the reason you've said this is to let your prospect know that you're committed to meeting his or her needs, it actually backfires. If you're not careful, you'll send the signal that you have nothing else going on, and that you need this prospect. This is an example of bad posture.

Even when the appointment time and date have been firmly set, be careful of cancellation setups. For example, if the prospect says, "Please call me in the morning to confirm our meeting," this is simply a ploy, most of the time, to give the prospect a way out. What it means is that if you call in the morning and he simply doesn't feel like answering the phone, this is his way of canceling the meeting.

To prevent this from happening, you can say, "I'm not sure I'll be able to do this because of a few other appointments I have, but I can assure you that I'm great at keeping meetings. I'll go ahead and block my calendar, and you can pretend I'm bringing you a $10,000 check so you won't forget our time. See you at 12:00." You can word this any way you want, but the point is simple. Don't get sucked into chasing or begging. Your response in this manner will also strengthen your posture within the mind of your prospect, thus helping you close the sale after the presentation.

Over the years, I have helped hundreds of salespeople perfect their understanding of the dominant thoughts they are creating and of the potential pitfalls of appointment setting. In many cases, these were the only pieces to the puzzle that had to be fixed. And in all cases, it revolutionized the quality of their appointments. The main thing for you to realize right now is that the dominant thought patterns you create as you're setting appointments must be thought through absolutely. No matter how good you get, there will be potential appointment pitfalls you have to deal with and, although they are simple, they are often overlooked.

Move the Marbles

Do you ever wonder if there is a way to guarantee your success? The final part of this chapter will give you just that. Let me put it this way: every top producer became a producer first. Before finally being recognized as someone at the top of his or her game, the top producer obviously had to conduct a certain number of presentations to get there. Although this number can change for everyone, it's not that drastically different. Under this logic, we can conclude that you *do* have a number. Your number may be 157, 243, or 551, but it is definitely there. What this number represents is simple. Remember, "Enough qualified appointments will always guarantee your success." With that said, we can conclude that your magic number is the exact number of qualified presentations it will take for you to make it to the top.

What I really want you to do is "move the marbles." As soon as you can, go out and purchase two glass jars, each at least two quarts in size. Then purchase 200 marbles. Place all 200 marbles in a jar labeled "Prospects," and label the empty jar "Qualified Appointments." The goal is simple. Move the 200 marbles from one jar to the other. Now let me pause here and interject a thought on urgency. The interesting thing about this scenario is that you can pick how fast you want to move the marbles from one jar to the other. You can move four to five per month for three and a half years, or you can move twenty per month for ten months. The speed is up to you. Whatever you do, don't try to beat the odds. Many salespeople begin this process, and somewhere around marble number fifteen, they know just enough to be dangerous. If they are not careful, they spend more energy trying to fix their system than actually working it. This has been the downfall for many who had great potential. There is, however, an answer—just move the marbles.

Now You Know

Your magic number is the exact number of qualified appointments it will take for you to make it to the top.

Generally speaking, the number 200 has had a major impact on the career of many a salesperson. That is why I use it. It seems never to fail. When people in direct sales show their 200th presentation, the same thing happens to them that happens to a real estate agent who shows his 200th home or an insurance agent who meets with her 200th prospective client to discuss a life insurance policy. These salespeople generally mastered all aspects of their system and now move among the elite in their company. With only a 20 percent closing ratio, they will have made forty-plus sales or closed forty-plus transactions. Because of the persistence they displayed, their self-esteem has increased. The fact that they didn't give up enhances their leadership ability, which generally reflects in the performance of their team.

In many cases, however, a salesperson begins the process of moving the marbles, but somewhere along the way, she loses the focus on her goal. She gets so hung up on her closing ratio or the next marketing strategy she believes will magically speed up her results, that she focuses on maximizing each and every marble instead of moving them from one jar to another. In essence, this salesperson is doing exactly what it takes to make it to the top of her industry, but she stopped doing what got her to where she currently is. She began to violate the Law of the Big Rocks, and she cut corners. She cut herself short of her rightful financial destiny.

Avoid all of this by simply continuing to move the marbles. *Now You Know* how moving the marbles can propel you to great heights within your company.

- If you want to reach the top level of your company—move the marbles!
- If you want to be employee of the month—move the marbles!
- If you want to master your system—move the marbles!
- If you want to become a leader in your industry—move the marbles!

I challenge you to move 200 marbles as fast as you can. Get radical. Get motivated. Get focused. Get ready to cash the checks!

Moving the marbles requires an understanding of what the big rocks are. Now that you know what qualified appointments are and how to set them, the only thing left to do is to set an aggressive goal. When you are filling your planner or daily schedule with qualified appointments (the big rocks), you can justifiably expect to achieve the results you are looking for. You may not hit every goal you set right away, but if you are tracking your progress, you will definitely see yourself coming closer to achieving the goal. I recommend that each qualified appointment represent a marble, and that you move 200 marbles as fast as you can. *Now You Know.*

CHAPTER 5

LAW V:
THE LAW OF EXPECTATIONS

*Your expectations
determine your closing ratio.*

I f there were a way to double your closing ratio, would you want
to know about it? Right now, you are probably saying to yourself,
"Of course!" You're probably also thinking, or perhaps hoping,
that this chapter will give you the exact phrases to use after you've
completed your presentation. I'm sorry to disappoint you, but this
assumption would be wrong. You see, there are countless books to
teach you the verbiage to use to close a sale. I'm sure the company
you represent has this type of literature and training available
as well. My experience, as someone who has trained and coun-
seled thousands of network marketers and salespeople across the
nation, is that you have already been taught the phrases to close

a sale, and if not, that information is available to you whenever you want it. There's a strong possibility that you have read and used closing phrases that you have been taught, but that they're just not getting results, and so you continue to seek new ideas, thinking that you will find a magic phrase to send you to the top of your game. In fact, this continual search for the answer to "how to close the deal" is causing you to perform below your full potential. The reality is that by the time you get to the end of your presentation, the deal is either closed or not. This reminds me of when Mohammed Ali said, in an interview, "I either won or lost the fight before I even entered the ring." Sure, there are things you can say to help get the paperwork out, but this part of the closing process is always trumped by the words and actions that have taken place throughout the entire process leading up to this point. This process reveals itself, for the most part, by the your expectations.

Let me share an experience I had to illustrate this point. My wife and I own a very expensive set of knives. As a matter of fact, they're the most expensive set of regular eating knives that I have ever heard of. To this day, I'm not sure how, or even why, we bought them. What I do know is that the salesperson expected to make the sale. She did this so well, in fact, that we ended up purchasing these knives that we neither wanted nor needed—and that we couldn't spare the money for at the time. I also know that the scissors that came with these knives will cut through a penny—really. The salesperson proved it right in front of me, with my penny.

I'll never forget that day. It started when I received a call from my wife letting me know that I should be at my office at a certain time for a presentation. I still remember the frustration of pulling in and seeing an unfamiliar vehicle parked in the lot. I entered the building to find an unfamiliar salesperson waiting for us. That moment is still imprinted clearly in my mind. I had initially told my wife that I was bogged down with deadlines and that I would not be able to attend the presentation, thinking to myself, "Whatever she's selling, Ryan, you're not buying!" Before I arrived, Jenny had assured me that this was just a favor for a friend, and that she wasn't planning to buy anything either. Little did I know, this was not the same plan this top salesperson had in her mind.

To ensure that I wasn't sucked into buying these knives that I didn't want and couldn't afford, I kindly told the salesperson that I had deadlines I had to meet and that I would be in the other room finishing up a project. She said she understood. I left Jenny to view the presentation alone. She was better at letting people down than I was, so it was the best scenario all around . . . or so I thought. From the other room, I couldn't help but overhear parts of the presentation. I was convinced that the salesperson was an obvious believer in her product. She conducted herself with a confident, matter-of-fact style, and she truly expected that anyone who saw this presentation would want what she was offering. The fact that she had prequalified the prospect (my wife), built belief through a third-party endorsement, and was giving a proven presentation that had already sold thousands of other sets of knives allowed her to take the position of strength, and assume that we must be as intelligent as the thousands of other previous knife purchasers had been. (I bet you could develop the same expectations based on the proven system with your company.) This sense of belief and understanding gave her the edge she needed, and after she demonstrated how strong the scissors were by cutting my penny in half, the only logical question to ask was, "Which set would you like to eat with tonight?" As she asked Jenny this question, she placed the application down in front of her, and with pen in hand, she asked the second question: "Would you like to pay for them in full, or would you prefer our easy payment plan?"

I do not believe that this salesperson made the sale after every presentation she did, but I do know that she dramatically increased her chances of closing the sale by the expectations she chose to believe in. On a side note, ten years after purchasing those knives, we're still eating with them. I also catch myself bragging about these knives quite a bit. Perhaps I'm still trying to justify the fact that we paid so much for them.

LAW #5, THE LAW OF EXPECTATIONS, STATES, "YOUR EXPECTATIONS DETERMINE YOUR CLOSING RATIO."

These expectations are derived from our belief systems, and they dictate the entire process of communication between you and your prospect. Expectations are beliefs.

In my home library, I have Brian Tracy's book *The Art of Closing the Sale*. This is one of my favorite books written on the subject, and I highly recommend it for every sales library. In the book, Brian says this about closing: "If you are completely fluent in closing and absolutely confident in your ability to ask for the order at the end of your sales presentation, you will be more aggressive about prospecting in the first place. You will have higher self-esteem and a better self-image. You will become more active each sales day, and you will even use your time better. Because you know that you can close the sale, you will feel like a winner most of the time." He also says, "The best news is that all sales skills, including closing, are learned and are learnable. If you can drive a car, you can learn how to close the sale."

Now You Know
Top producers in sales assume that everyone is a sale. They simply assume that their prospect is going to get involved in some way.

Core Expectations

In this chapter, we will address the core beliefs about closing that will allow you to expect the close through the entire process of your sale, ultimately increasing your closing ratio. In any sales team, the greatest leaders are the best closers. If it is your desire to have a team of people following you, closing the sale may be the single biggest skill you ever develop to get people to buy into your leadership. Even if much of your time is spent helping others close their sales, an air of competence, professionalism, and inspiration is derived from those who work with someone who can help them accomplish their goals. I'm not saying that you will have to close everyone, but if you can learn to close the sale a decent percentage of the time, you will instill confidence within your team members and provide them with enough belief to keep them going until they develop their own abilities to close and lead others. For this to happen, you have to develop a strong core belief system about closing, and it begins with the following core beliefs.

Core Expectation #1: Everyone is a sale.

If you recall what we talked about in Law #1, the Law of the First Impression, you will remember that the close begins in the first thirty seconds. With that thought in mind, we can conclude that certain closing expectations need to take place throughout the entire process—not just at the end of the transaction. Top producers in sales expect that everyone is a sale. We all know that, in reality, everyone is not going to be a sale, but because these sales professionals have that expectation, and because they act on that expectation throughout their entire presentation, they say things that direct their prospect toward buying their product from the moment they open their mouths until the transaction is complete. Top producers simply expect that their prospect is going to get involved in some way. And because they expect, they tend to handle themselves differently. This is the foundational belief from which everything in this chapter builds.

Of course, they've learned certain closing statements, but if that's all there is to closing then we could just print these statements, memorize them, and everyone in sales would be great closers, right? Wrong. It just doesn't work this way. Yes, there are certain words, or statements, that can help keep you on track (we will go over some of these), but it's the "expectation attitude" that I want to teach you.

Core Expectation #2: You are an interviewer, not a salesperson.

The best way for you to improve your closing ratio is to approach every sale as if you are an interviewer and your prospects are the interviewee. Let's start by taking a look at the interview process. Most salespeople approach their prospect as if they have something they are trying to sell. They spend most of their time trying to figure out ways (or angles) to approach their prospect and weave themselves into an appointment. Although many do get appointments with this mindset, the "throw mud against a wall and see if any sticks" approach is ineffective for anyone who wants huge success. What if you created a mindset where you were in charge of who bought or didn't buy your product? What if you asked all the right questions of your prospect, which ultimately led him down a certain pattern of thinking, and finally to the answer you were hoping for? That answer is your product or company. This is what the professionals do. Your success begins with developing the mindset of an interviewer and not an interviewee.

Imagine the following scenario: You are working for a company, and they ask you to hire at least two competent individuals to fill an important position. These individuals need to be hired by next week. Let's look at what takes place. First, you or your assistant runs an ad online and/or in local newspapers. Next, as calls begin to come in, you set up interview appointments. You prepare a series of questions, and on the day of the interview, you ask those questions. Based on the answers you receive, you begin to formulate your opinions of the interviewees. You judge them on the content of their answers, their personalities, and their reactions to whatever it is you throw their way. After ten to twenty of these interviews, you begin the selection process. Your goal now is to select the best possible candidates for the two positions.

How does this relate to sales? I'm not suggesting that you interview your prospects exactly like you would if you were thinking about hiring them for a job, but what I am suggesting is that you develop the mindset of an interviewer. If you were the interviewer at this place of business, what would you do if the person wanting the job showed up thirty minutes late for the interview? What if he cursed three or four times throughout the interview? What if you really liked him and wanted to hire him, but he wouldn't return your call? What would you do? The answer is *nothing*. The reality is that you probably wouldn't lose much sleep at all. This is the mindset you want to possess to be a great closer. You never want to be emotionally tied to the outcome of any decision that any prospect will make.

To further your understanding of this closing expectation, let me explain how you can avoid ever hearing the word no. I didn't say never *get* a no, just never *hear* it. Think of your sales system as a funneling system—again, one that has been proven to work for many top leaders in your company and/or industry. Once you develop the interviewer attitude, the funneling system could go like this: You prequalified your prospect, and she seems like she is interested, so you set the appointment. On the day of the appointment, your prospect doesn't show up—she doesn't even call. The worst part is that the appointment was at her house, which you drove an hour and a half to get to. Of course you should do a follow-up call and find out whether there was a legitimate reason for the cancellation, but if you have an interviewer's mindset, this prospect already has one strike against her. Your thinking should be that she is not qualified to work with you because she missed an appointment and did not call you to reschedule. Most novice salespeople would now become frustrated and start calling the prospect repeatedly, thus making themselves come across as being desperate. You know that this is considered bad posture. Let's say you finally get ahold of the prospect, and she tells you she is not interested. Again, if you approach the process as if you are the interviewer, you will not be that upset because you've already decided she didn't qualify to work with you in the first place. In essence, you told her no before she told you no. The interviewer always has the edge.

Now You Know

The interviewer always has the edge. If you tell the prospect no first, then you'll never really hear him or her say no.

If you tell the prospect no first, then you'll never really hear him or her say no. If this seems like a mind game, that's because it is. You are psychologically setting yourself up to be able to withstand the emotional storm of the highs and lows. In addition, this attitude is a major part of expecting the close. After you've attained the top level in your company, you will look back and see that this was one of the biggest reasons you made it. It's simple—without emotional stability, there can be no long-term focus. Disclaimer: Don't make the mistake of thinking you should be out there looking to disqualify prospects. Just be aware of what your prospect is saying and doing so you don't waste time "chasing" the wrong people.

Core Expectation #3: You have to ask the right questions to get the right answers.

We determine the value of our time, and the questions we ask about whom we spend time with dictate this value. All sales systems are designed to prequalify, build belief, set appointments, show presentations, and close sales. Very few, however, emphasize the permission to create standards of excellence with those to whom you present. Maybe this way of thinking is only for those who wish to have large bank accounts. Obviously, if we strengthen the quality of our appointments (Law #4), our closing ratio has to go up. The following four questions are designed to help you decide whether your prospect is even closeable before you start to close.

1. *Does my prospect really want to be here, listening?* This is an important question to ask. An honest answer will inform you whether you are prequalifying your prospects the correct way. If you go through a series of presentations during which your prospects are distracted and are constantly doing things like answering their phones or looking at notes from a previous meeting, then you have a problem that should be fixed on the front end.

2. *Has my prospect been presented with enough third-party endorsements?* Although each company is different in this regard, you should never underestimate the power of third-party testimonies. We will discuss this later in the chapter.

3. *Is my prospect the decision maker?* We talked about this in chapter 2, but it's worth mentioning again. If most of your presentations end with the prospect's response, "I'll have to talk with my husband [or wife] before I make a decision," then you are falling into the trap of showing your business or product to the person who isn't the decision maker in the household. If you hear, "I'll have to run this by my boss," then either you're not reaching the decision maker, or your sales cycle is complex, and you will have to face more than one decision maker. Most of the time, the problem is that you're meeting with the wrong person; however, in a longer sales cycle, you may find that there are several decision makers

and a hierarchy to navigate. There will be times when you may have to make multiple presentations. It can become frustrating, but don't give up!

4. *Can the prospect afford what I am selling?* This one is a little tricky in that it is typically not good to prejudge anyone, but if you are selling a product that is high end and you are constantly dealing with individuals who say they can't afford your product, then maybe you should get tighter on the front end of the screening process. Sometimes it's simply not possible for your prospect to afford your product, and you have to move on.

Answering these four questions will not guarantee the sale, but it will cause you to increase the quality of your appointments so you can increase your results in closing the sale. I found that once I learned how to fill my calendar with appointments, the only way I could increase my productivity was to learn how to get pickier about who I spent time with. These questions helped me so much that when I arrived at a presentation, the sale was 70 percent closed before I started.

Core Expectation #4: It's hard for your prospect not to say yes.

Everyone wants to say yes (well, mostly everyone). Even those who don't have the money want to say yes. This is why they avoid you when they have to say no. They don't like the feeling. As interesting as this topic is, we can use the power of this human tendency to direct a yes, even when it otherwise might have been a no.

One key way to do this is to incorporate "yes statements" into your vocabulary. If you can learn to incorporate four to six yes statements into your presentation, when it comes time for your prospect to say yes to buying your product or filling out the application, it is much easier because he has already said yes several times. For example, let's say that after you present one of the many logical reasons why he should own your product, you pause and say, "Now that just makes sense doesn't it?" Even if your prospect refrains from answering aloud, if it was said correctly, he will be thinking, "Yes." Learning to communicate this way will also enable you to have a greater impact on your connection with your prospect.

Now You Know

A successful presenter moves people to action by being relatable through personal stories or third-party testimonies.

Core Expectation #5: Closing the sale is nothing more than overcoming objections.

In his book, Brian Tracy says, "Objections indicate interest. The fact is if there are no objections, there is no interest. If there is no interest, there will be no sale." In this section, I will illustrate how you can use what I call "The Box" throughout your sales process to overcome objections before they even surface and to squelch the objections that do come up. Using this technique is a surefire way to increase your chance of making the sale.

Mastering The Box is the best way I know of to become a power closer. I call this The Box because a prospect's job is to try to find a way out of making a commitment. She wants to get out of The Box of commitment. (It's not her fault. She can't help it. That's just the way many people are programmed.) A prospect can escape any commitment by using simple objections and disguising them as legitimate reasons. In a box, there are six sides. What I like to do is build five of those walls throughout my presentation, walls that emotionally and logically eliminate the prospect's objections through reasoning, thus building a box that has only one exit—the close.

One of the best ways to overcome objections regarding your product or company is to identify the five most common objections that your market will usually present beforehand and then address them in a way that offers solutions throughout your presentation. Think about the most effective presenters you have watched throughout your time in the sales industry. I am sure those people have a knack for addressing objections within their presentation. Everyone thinks that he or she is extremely talented at presenting, and there's no doubt some are, but a successful presenter who moves people to action has mastered the art of being relatable either through personal stories or third-party testimonies that offer simple solutions to most objections.

Analyze the most common objections you might deal with, and learn how to weave illustrations that overcome these objections throughout your presentation. In direct sales, for example, the top five excuses you might hear the most may be these: not enough time, don't have the money, don't like sales, don't like to stock products, and don't know anyone.

Take a moment to write down the top five objections you receive when you attempt to close the sale:

1. _____
2. _____
3. _____
4. _____
5. _____

Are you addressing these issues throughout your presentation? Next time you watch a top presenter in your company, take notice of how he uses personal stories or third-party facts to address these issues. He may not even know he is doing this, but he is. All of these types of objections—and more—can be dealt with throughout your presentation, thus resulting in a "nowhere else to go" scenario for your prospect—The Box.

"Expectation" Statements, Phrases, and Concepts

In addition to the concept of The Box, there are certain statements, phrases, and concepts you can use to help create a more natural closing scenario. Learning to use these statements, phrases, and concepts properly can help you effectively navigate your way through many different types of scenarios and achieve your desired results. Below are five examples.

Example 1: The word "obviously."
The most powerful closing word you can use is *obviously*.

When prequalifying your prospect, begin to generate interest. After using one of your proven tools (such as a pamphlet, magazine, CD, DVD, or online video), you might say, "Well, Bob, *obviously* that wasn't enough information for you to make a decision. The next step is to get you some more information." This stops your prospect from deciding yes or no and subliminally directs him toward how you want him to be thinking.

Let's say you run into a prospect on the street and hand him an audio. The next day, you call that prospect, clear his time, and say something like, "That was a great audio wasn't it?" It doesn't matter what the answer is, or even if he listened to the information. The next sentence out of your mouth is, "*Obviously*, you would need to have some more information to make a decision. Why don't we grab lunch and talk over the details?" The key here is to book the appointment.

Let's say you truly have an interested prospect, and you would like to set an appointment for her to get the details, but she begins to start asking questions. You obviously don't want to break Law #2 (you see how I just used the word); instead, after her questions, you reply with, "*Obviously*, you would need to look at the details before you could make a decision. So why don't we get together so you can get all the information you'll need? What night is better for you—Monday or Tuesday?"

Let's say that after your presentation, you're looking for a statement to begin the closing process. You could say, "Now *obviously*, there's no way anyone could lose." Or, "*Obviously*, this makes sense, because even if you didn't want to make money with our company as a distributor, you can see the value that our product offers you." Or, "*Obviously* there is no reason not to fill out the paperwork tonight." If you use this word correctly, your prospect will be thinking, "Well, *obviously*." This occurs because he or she has felt the assumption that your product makes sense throughout your presentation.

Example 2: The statement "The Scale from 1 to 10 . . ."

This technique is an almost guaranteed way to get objections on the table. If overcoming objections is the key to closing the sale, then learning to get the objections on the table is a skill you need to master. Of all the methods I've used to get my prospect's objections on the table, the scale from 1 to 10 method has proven to be the most profitable.

Now You Know

Are you ready for the strongest closing tool you will ever develop? Silence is the ultimate power in assumption.

Here is how it works: After your presentation, begin by asking this simple question: "Bob, obviously this makes sense, but let me go ahead and ask you, *on a scale from 1 to 10*, one not being interested, and ten being ready to participate tonight, where do you see yourself?"

Now this communicates an expectation. You're expecting that he likes what he is seeing. He may say a seven or an eight, or he might say a four or a five. If he says anything lower than a seven, then you've got your work cut out for you. Typically, in this instance, I provide additional testimonies so I can increase his belief. It could be a money problem, or it could be something he's not telling you. Either way, the question will let you know where you are. If he says a seven or higher, then he is probably closeable that night. If that's the case, your next question should be, "What questions do I need to answer tonight to get you from an eight to a ten?"

At this point, I would like to address the strongest closing tool you will ever develop.

Example 3: The concept of Silence.

Silence is the ultimate power in closing the sale. It took

me many years to learn the power of silence in closing the sale. Most salespeople fail to understand silence. The novice tries to fill these gaps either by offering more information about the product or by stressing the reasons he or she thinks the prospect should purchase the product. The prospect never has time to make a decision because the novice is too busy selling! When you master the use of silence after asking a question of expectation, you actually send a message of confidence to your prospect that says, "I'm so confident in any scenario you present to me that you might as well go ahead and give in now."

Let's revisit and finish the scenario we discussed in the earlier paragraph. After asking your prospect, "What questions do I need to answer tonight to get you from an eight to a ten?" sit and wait for the answer. You may have to wait fifteen to thirty seconds, but understand that he who speaks first loses. Eventually, with this method, your prospects will set themselves up to be closed. Now remember, this does not mean you will close everyone, but the understanding and perfection of this law will play a key role in helping you reach the top of your game. If the prospect answers with any kind of objection that can be answered that night, then it's time to expect that you can overcome the objection quickly and close the deal. The best way I found to move your prospect closer to a decision is to use the three simple words in example four.

Example 4: The Statement, "Other than that . . ."

This is one of the most powerful closing phrases you can use. Let's say that the answer to the question ended up being, "Well I need to get some quotes." Or, "If it's so good, why haven't I heard about this product yet?"

A statement that projects the proper expectation could be, *"Other than that*, is there anything stopping you from purchasing tonight?" Or, *"Other than that*, is there anything stopping us from filling out the paperwork out this evening?"

Your prospect might say, "Well, I'm not sure how I'm going to pay for it." You can respond with, "Okay, *other than that*, is there anything stopping you from filling out the paperwork tonight?"

You can use *other than that* until you get to the bottom line or until you determine that the sale is not going to happen. In most cases, though, when you get to this point in your presentation, it is paramount that you do the following: get out your applications and expect that the prospect wants what you have. Oh, and by the way, you *must* have applications. As funny as it sounds, many salespeople are so *unexpecting* that they don't even bring applications with them to the presentation. Funny, but true.

You may still have an objection or two to overcome, but using statements that project proper expectations will allow you to close a much higher percentage of sales.

Example 5: Concept —The power of third-party documentation.

One final thought about overcoming objections is that you can always use third-party documentation and/or testimonies to help answer any questions. Testimonies are one of the most powerful tools you can use to help build belief and close deals. In the direct-selling industry, and in most sales systems, the use of third-party documentation and testimonies can play a vital part in your success.

Now You Know that expecting the close is an attitude and that, as a sales professional, if you take the time to learn the techniques outlined in this chapter, you will always double your chances of making a sale. And *Now You Know* how to initiate the final close by using expecting statements.

Did you know that the majority of the people who purchase books never make it past the first chapter? Amazing, isn't it? When they purchase a book, they have every intention of reading it. With regard to *Now You Know*, you are expecting to learn how to become a more productive sales professional. But, in many cases, books end up doing nothing more collecting dust on a bookshelf somewhere. With that said, I want to congratulate you for making it this far. It tells me that you are serious about increasing your productivity and income. I commend you for being a person who finishes what he or she starts. Now, as a bonus, it's time to move into my favorite sections of the book—chapters 6 and 7—to address how we create sales momentum.

CHAPTER 6

LAW VI:
THE LAW OF THE 80/20 RULE

If you fail 80 percent of the time long enough—you win!

Have you ever met someone who changed your life? I had the fortunate opportunity to know and work with former drag racing professional, Dick Loehr. Dick began his career as a young man heading up Ford's drag racing team in the late '60s. From there, he went on to own and operate car dealerships with nine different franchises. Dick was handpicked by Lee Iacocca to serve on a board that helped turn Chrysler around—one of the largest turnarounds in corporate history. Dick also served on the Statue of Liberty Restoration Committee. Later in life, he founded a Fort Lauderdale-based direct-sales company. When I met Dick, he was in his late fifties, and I was in my mid-twenties. Somehow, we made a connection, and he ended up becoming a key mentor in my life. One of the many topics we discussed frequently was the 80/20 rule. He used to say to me, "Boy (that is what he called me), I don't care what it is you do, the 80/20 rule can't be broken." He mainly said this when I was would discuss the frustrations I was having in building my sales team. I can still hear his voice on a regular basis and see his quiet chuckle as if he continues to make this point to me: "If you fail 80 percent of the time long enough—you win!" Even though his life on Earth has ended, his legacy has not.

The 80/20 Rule has a few other names. It has also been called the Law of the Vital Few and the Pareto Principle, which was named after Italian economist Vilfredo Pareto, who observed in 1906 that 80 percent of the land in Italy was owned by 20 percent of the population. Pareto further developed the principle by observing that 20 percent of the peapods in his garden contained 80 percent of the peas. Today, it has become a common rule of thumb in business.

The 80/20 Rule states that 80 percent of our productivity comes from about 20 percent of our efforts. You could relate this rule to many areas of life. For example, you could say that 80 percent of the work in your church comes from about 20 percent of the congregation, or that 80 percent of the sales in your organization come from about 20 percent of the salespeople. However you use it, the 80/20 Rule does exist, and seems to work itself out in an uncanny way.

In this chapter, I want to explain a law that, once understood, will be the foundation for any momentum you will ever create in a sales career. It is a law that will propel your business to great heights when applied and that will severely stifle your growth and income when broken. Law #6 is really a law about momentum.

LAW #6, THE LAW OF THE 80/20 RULE, STATES, "IF YOU FAIL 80 PERCENT OF THE TIME LONG ENOUGH—YOU WIN!"

Let's say you want to reach the top sales level in your company. It is common sense that if you set enough qualified appointments, and fail 80% of the time long enough, that the 20% success ratio will eventually cause you reach your goal.

To understand the 80/20 Rule in sales, you really need a deep understanding of the numbers game. It is my experience that if I ask 100 salespeople if they know that sales is a numbers game, 95 of them will say, "Absolutely!" Unfortunately, 95 percent of them are either inadvertently lying to themselves, or they aren't willing to do what they know it takes to be successful. Think about it. If they claim to understand that selling is a numbers game, then why doesn't their activity level reflect that belief? If reaching the top is a result of going through the numbers, then it would appear that the majority of sales professionals are just choosing not to be successful. Now I certainly don't think that people are lying, but I do believe that they do not fully understand the numbers game. I am hoping that the following illustration will provide you with a new awareness and understanding of what could possibly take place in your business and life. I also hope that this newly applied philosophy of Law #6, coupled with a firm commitment to not break this law, will result in the foundation for true momentum within your sales career.

In 1995, I took a job as a collector for a subprime finance company in central Florida. This was the first job I took right after I married my beautiful wife Jenny. It was at this job that I learned how to make 50 to 100 difficult and negative sales calls every day. I say that because these calls were primarily to individuals who didn't have any money, needed their cars, and were behind on their bills. I was calling to remind them that they were late on their payments (as if they needed me to remind them). Needless to say, they were not happy to hear my voice. What they didn't know was that most of them were doing better financially than I was. You have to imagine this: Here I am, Ryan Chamberlin, behind on everything that I was making payments on, which was everything. I'm going to work every day, calling people on the phone to collect money from them. Then I go home and check my answering machine, only to discover messages from other bill collectors. Because I have always been the type of guy who tries to learn from every experience, there were times when I would actually take out my pad and pen and take notes. Those messages on my answering machine gave me some of my best material. It's ironic, but you could say this was my continual training program.

One of the most memorable experiences about this job happened to me the very first day I was hired. My boss shook my hand and handed me a box of about 500 stock business cards. He asked me to type my name on about 100 of them. This is how much he believed in his employees. It was not exactly a self-esteem booster. My boss's actions sent the message to me that he didn't think I would be there very long. Have you ever tried to type your name on a business card? I couldn't even line the card up in a type-writer. As if that weren't bad enough, my boss wanted me to use my own ink. And if that's not bad enough, have you ever handed a hand-typed business card to someone you're trying to impress? It doesn't work so well. I doubt anyone I handed my hand-typed business card to ever took me seriously.

What I really learned from this job was the numbers game. Day after day, I made 50 to 100 calls. Some days were better than others, but as far as the numbers were concerned, the only way I didn't meet my goal was if I didn't make the calls. Some days, I would have a 95 percent failure ratio in getting ahold of people or collecting money. Other days, it seemed like 50 percent. Overall, it averaged out. For me to be able to do this day in and day out, there was a trick. I had to learn how to take the emotion out of the task. Don't be confused into thinking I was never passionate or aggressive; I just mean that I was able to master the ability to take the emotions out of the *outcome* and put all my emotions into the *process*. When you give the process everything you have, then all that's left to do is to deal with the outcome—good or bad.

Understanding Momentum

Momentum in sales continues with an understanding of what we get paid for. Consider the following example: Let's say that when you make ten sales or recruit ten people into your business, you generate $2,000. If your prospect–to–close ratio is 80/20, meaning that of every ten prospects you prequalify with your system, you end up with two sales, then it is understandable that you need to funnel fifty people through your system to end up with ten sales. In this scenario, you ultimately end up with forty no's and ten yes's. Let me ask you this all-important question: What do you really get paid for? Is it the yes's, or is it the no's?

The answer is neither.

What you really get paid for is the fifty prospects. You see, there is no way to determine whether any of the fifty prospects will convert into sales. What you can do is count on the 80/20. You obviously need to adjust these numbers to reflect the 80/20 rule as it works out in your personal business, but I can almost guarantee that you'll come up with a similar ratio.

Follow me with the continuation of our previous discussion. If you earn $2,000 for ten sales, and what you are actually getting paid for is bringing fifty prospects through your system, then it actually breaks down to $40 per prospect, whether each is a yes or a no. In fact, if you multiply it out, you would really be getting paid $400 for the yes's and $1,600 for the no's. Furthermore, if you truly understand the numbers game, then you'd have to understand that you get paid more for the no's than you do the yes's. With this way of thinking, you can literally get excited about hearing the word no!

Now You Know
If you truly understand the numbers game, then you understand that you get paid more for the no's than you do the yes's!

How to Not Let Your Emotions Affect Your Performance
Most people break Law #6 when they overanalyze their no's to the point that it affects their emotions. This results in lower performance. When performance is affected, momentum is lost. The fact is that in the majority of cases, salespeople never get to the point where

their pipeline is full enough to allow the 80/20 rule to work in their favor. (A pipeline is a system in which you organize all the prospects that you are currently working with. Try to visualize a pipe where, if you put enough in, something has to come out on the other side. It's also similar to a baseball diamond, meaning that when the bases are loaded and the batter gets a hit, someone is going to score.) As a result, they are in constant violation of Law #6. They violate this law because of their incorrect expectation of the results they think they should be getting based on the amount of work they are doing. They become frustrated with the fact that they didn't close their last two sales, but they ignore the fact that they didn't communicate with ten prospects. In other words, they didn't do the work to justify the results they are looking for. Because of this incorrect expectation, not only is their level of action affected, but their performance is also tainted because their posture is affected to the point that no matter what they do with their simple, proven, or even guaranteed system, it doesn't seem to work.

This can all be fixed by keeping a pipeline full enough to allow the 80/20 rule to constantly perform. If someone is trying to make two sales per week, for example, they should not focus on the two sales as much as they should with the ten prospects. Keeping the pipeline full of this kind of activity will always result in a higher percentage of closing. Lastly, this type of performance based thinking can literally help you determine how much, and how fast, you want to succeed.

I would like to leave you with this thought about the top producers in your company. They are the biggest failures you know! Wait— don't close the book. This is not a negative statement. The top producers in your company have failed more than anyone else in your company, which is why they are more successful that anyone else in your company. They should be your heroes. Not because they failed, but because they persevered and proved to you that if you fail enough, you *will* reach the top. To succeed, you must not fear failure. The only real failure in life is the failure to continue to try. Take Michael Jordan, for example. In an interview, this is what Jordan said about failing: "I missed 9,000 shots in my career. I've lost almost 300 games. Twenty-six times I've been entrusted to take the game-winning shot and missed. I've failed over and over and over again in my life. And that is why I succeeded."

Now You Know

It's simply a fact that you have to fail long enough. Remember, if you fail 80 percent of the time long enough, you will eventually hit every goal you set.

If you are working and struggling, you are winning. It may not feel like it, but you are on your way to victory—as long as you persist.

I realize that because you have taken the time to read this book, you may have committed to your system for a week, a month, or possibly even a year or more. You may have made a few sales that created some excitement. If you are like many sales professionals, these sales may have been followed by two or three weeks during which you spoke with a handful of prospects and didn't make any sales. You were living the 80/20 rule. The problem arises when you don't understand it and stop. You may have started to second-guess yourself. Everyone does this, but top money earners conclude by developing an understanding of the numbers game.

In most cases, if you care enough about your career to read this book, at some point you were doing everything it took to be a top producer. You did exactly what was needed. Maybe you just didn't do it long enough. This law cannot work without consistency. Working any system for a week or two and then stopping to rest before starting and stopping again and again will not work—with any company or with any product. It's simply a fact that you have to fail long enough.

Remember, if you fail 80 percent of the time long enough, you will eventually hit every goal you set. *Now You Know* why sales is a numbers game and that if you fail long enough—you win!

CHAPTER 7

LAW VII:
THE LAW OF URGENCY

The speed at which you pursue your goals and dreams affects everything!

Don't you hate it when you're running late for the airport, and it seems that everyone around you is moving slower than normal? During moments like these, you think most of the people you come in contact with have no urgency about their day. They obviously don't care that you are running late, and they seem to be trying to sabotage your 3:47 flight to Atlanta. It can be one of the most frustrating things to deal with in life. I have actually found myself wanting to honk my horn at a person in front of me because he is only doing 20 miles per hour over the speed limit. Why? Because I have a destination I need to get to, and I am passionate about doing so sooner rather than later. In sales, if you know where you want to go and have a deadline to get there, you can create that same sense of urgency—only this time, you won't miss your flight. But you will, because of the effects of the Law of Urgency, be able to afford a first-class ticket.

As we venture into the final law, let me share with you a personal story of how urgency changed my life. I'll never forget the mental state I was in the day I came home, and my wife told me that a former business partner had left a message on our answering machine. He said that he had an opportunity he wanted me to look at. He was able to capture my curiosity, and because we hadn't seen each other in more than a year, I agreed to meet. This was partly because I was at a place in my life where I was looking for an opportunity. In addition, by now I had developed a reputation as a hard worker, but my efforts had left me with little to nothing to show for it. As a matter of fact, my financial position during this period was worse than it had been since I graduated from high school seven years earlier. Now, at the age of twenty-five, I was married and had a child, I had worked hard for other people for years, and I simply wasn't satisfied. I had tried several sales positions and failed. I even opened my own business and failed. I was behind on every bill I had. My interest was starting to accumulate interest. You could say that I was desperate, and for the first time in my life, I was faced with an overwhelming sense that I needed to make drastic changes—and I needed them to happen fast.

The good news is that I was looking at a new opportunity, and the bad news (I thought) is that it was in sales. Luckily, though, there was a mentor within this sales company who was willing to coach me on what has evolved into these seven laws. I just had to bring three things to the table. I was to have a burning desire, be teachable, and be willing to do the work. I committed to these success requirements by saying to my mentor, "Tell me what I have to do, and I'll do it." After his counsel, I immediately began to apply the concepts in this chapter as I worked my new sales opportunity with extreme urgency. Most active salespeople in the company were doing two to three presentations per week; I was booking two to three per day. Over the next several months, with this newfound urgency, I accelerated my understanding and development of the other six laws. Practically overnight, I went from just getting by financially to earning more money every month than I had previously earned in a year. In addition, my self-worth was on the rise, and ultimately this law served as a catalyst for balanced success in other areas of my life. I'm far from perfect, but as you read the rest of this chapter, you'll gain an understanding of what I believe will happen to anyone who applies the Law of Urgency to his or her life.

LAW #7, THE LAW OF URGENCY, STATES, "THE SPEED AT WHICH YOU PURSUE YOUR GOALS AFFECTS EVERYTHING!"

Urgency, according to this book, is simply the speed at which you pursue your goals and dreams. Somehow, this individual pursuit for urgency is transmitted to your prospect. In many cases, if you possess true urgency, your prospect will feel compelled to be a part of your plan, and even if he doesn't buy your product, he may refer you to someone who will—and he may become a customer at a later time. Nevertheless, he will have felt the power of urgency from someone with a purpose. Urgency has an almost mystical ability to become a magnetic force that enables you to attract the success you're looking for. For this reason, we will study three core ingredients that help create a sense of urgency. We begin with your *why*.

Core Ingredient One: A Sense of Urgency—Your "Why"
In my opinion, urgency is developed within you when your *why* is clearly defined. The clearer the reason you are pursuing your particular goals and dreams, the more of an effect it will have on the outcome of your career. Your reason could be the desire for financial security, the ability to contribute to your church or charity, more time to enjoy with your family, or simply the want of certain material things that will enable you to enjoy an enriched lifestyle.

The bottom line is that if you show me a salesperson who doesn't know what she wants, I'll show you a calendar that's not full, follow-ups that aren't being done in a timely manner, sales trainings that are being missed, and laws that are consistently being broken. In his book *Strategic Acceleration*, the world-renowned coach for many of the most successful entrepreneurs of our time, Tony Jeary, tackles this topic with his teaching method of clarity, focus, and execution. Jeary writes, "Clarity actually provides a specific kind of power whose absence is painful, for it's manifested in human performance. In any endeavor, certain intangible human qualities must drive the effort. People have to believe in what they are doing. They must be committed to achievement. There must be a certain amount of mental toughness and resilience to persevere through difficulties and roadblocks. A certain amount of legitimate excitement never hurts, either. True clarity contributes to creating all these qualities, and with these qualities comes power—the power to produce results."

Core Ingredient Two: The Power of Recognition

To encourage urgency and the manifestation of clarity, focus, and execution, many sales organizations have wisely chosen to use recognition as one of their most powerful tools. I have discovered that many people will work harder for a fifteen-cent ribbon than they will for the $1,000 bonus that comes with it. Although this sounds humorous when you read it, look back over your career and take notice of when you performed at your highest levels. I bet you were striving for some kind of goal for which you would ultimately be recognized. And although you and I can attempt to argue that we are different, the truth is that there is a certain reaction humans have when it comes to recognition. Let's say it's a new house you are striving for instead of a level of achievement within your company. We could argue that you are focused on your goals with urgency because you want that house. I would dare to say, though, that as humans, we would all be lying if we weren't somewhat looking forward to the satisfaction that comes when the people closest to us discover that we have enough money to purchase a much nicer home. We may even throw ourselves a house-warming party just so all of our friends can see it. The desire for recognition catches us all, just sometimes in different ways.

If you are in the business of leading a team, you can use the power of recognition to create urgency within your sales organization. Often, recognition comes with a deadline, and the deadline coupled with a desirable reward is what helps create the urgency. If a new promotion developed in your organization is promoted vigorously, that alone can be the catalyst for momentum. It is been said that one of the largest privately owned life insurance companies in the world was built by giving away T-shirts to its highest performers every month. The owner of the company placed so much emphasis on that reward—and created such a culture within his company—that everyone wanted that T-shirt, and the only way to get one was to perform at a higher level.

Now You Know
If you are in the business of leading a team, you can use the power of recognition to create urgency within your sales organization.

Core Ingredient Three: The Compression Effect

The compression effect is when you take a large amount of activity and complete it in a short amount of time. This compressed activity creates the emotional ingredients that fuel momentum. As obvious as this seems, a lack of urgency in this area is often the result of an incorrect belief system. This, in turn, messes with our level of expectation and ultimately deteriorates our actions. The good news, however, is that this can all be corrected with a few adjustments to how we think.

Not too long ago, I was counseling with a new salesperson who was frustrated. He was frustrated because he wasn't getting the results he wanted. Summarizing the situation, he had been pursuing his new sales career for about six weeks. In this period, he had made two sales and had taken eight prospects through the funnel system. (Interesting, isn't it, that he was performing better than the 80/20 rule?) The frustrating part to him was that he had only made two sales in a month and a half. He was obviously ready to quit. As we discussed the situation, I asked him a series of questions. First, I asked, "About how long does it take to move one prospect through all the steps of your system?" We concluded that one and a half hours was plenty of time. Next, I made this statement: "So you've invested about twelve hours [eight times 1.5 hours] into your business in a month and a half?" At this point, his demeanor began to change as the realization of activity vs. productivity started to show itself.

I then said, "You know, most companies have at least two days, or sixteen hours, of orientation you'd have to go through. So we could say that you haven't even gotten through orientation, yet you're already frustrated." We both laughed at that one. I made my final point by saying, "You know, it is possible to do eight presentations in two days, wouldn't you agree?" He was careful not to answer yet, so I continued: "I mean, if your company were running a two-day special during which they were paying bonuses of $1,000 per presentation, how many presentations would you do in those two days?" There was silence. I pressed forward. "Would you only do one, or none, or would you try to do as many as you possibly could?"

He responded, "Now that you put it that way, if I were getting paid like that, I definitely could do more." (What he didn't realize here is that he trapped himself.) I then pointed out, "Okay, so that means if you could do four or more presentations per day for the bonus of $1,000 each, then you could do it for $0, right?" He agreed. I asked, "Now, if you would have done eight presentations in your first two days and made two sales during that period, would you have been excited?"

He responded with, "I think I get your point." And here it is ladies and gentlemen: you can complete the same number of sales presentations over different periods of time and get completely different outcomes, both psychologically and in the end results.

In this example, if this salesperson had done eight presentations in two days, he would have been ecstatic with the results. Instead, he took what he could have done in two days and spread it out over six weeks. The results were depressing. This individual never really had a first impression problem. He also didn't have staying-in-control, takeaway, appointment, closing, or pipeline (80/20) problems. The whole time, he simply had an *urgency* problem. The moral of the story is that if you take what you could do and make it take longer than it should, you warp the results you would have gotten. Finally, if you take a large amount of work and compress it into a short amount of time, you always create momentum. The length of time during which you keep up the urgency determines the total amount of momentum, but you will always create momentum with urgency.

Once you understand this illustration, we can conclude that most people have somewhat of an understanding of what work needs to be done to create momentum within their businesses. This leads me to this statement: I believe that most people already know what to do or know where they can learn what to do to create momentum within their sales businesses. And now that you know the core ingredients for urgency in sales, you can master them and find that urgency affects everything.

The Urgency Effects
Here are five examples of how urgency can affect all areas of your business.

The Urgency Effect #1: Emotional vs. Logical
The reality is simple. When emotions kick in, all logic goes out the door. Let's take, for example, the salesperson who attends his company training, has his goals laid out, and is ready to hit the ground running. Everywhere I go to train people on how to create momentum in their business, I get people to buy into the idea that there is a certain number of presentations that, if done consistently, can practically guarantee their success. For example, let's say you're in the direct-sales industry and your goal is to build two or three teams of business to secure your income. It's logical to come to the realization that if you show your presentation three to five times per week over the period of one year, you can expect to have several large teams established, which enables you to earn that passive income you desire.

If you do 150 to 250 presentations (move the marbles) with any business or any product, you're bound not only to generate a large amount of money, but also to become a professional during the process. This form of logic usually generates an agreement from anyone who analyzes his or her opportunity thoroughly. The problem is that although everyone *knows* what to do, very few ever do it. Why? Because emotions come into play!

When you leave your seminar or training, you have every intention of doing just what I've described, right? Then why haven't you? The problem for most occurs right after the first week—the week when they set their plans in motion, when they start receiving the no's or not receiving return phone calls or being rejected by their friends. They don't like the feelings they have, and sooner or later, logic is thrown out the door. They may have done three or four presentations and, in reality, they were on track with the 80/20 rule as taught in Law #6. If they had remained consistent, they would have hit their goals, but they never get there because they stopped. Again, it's logical to assume that if they had kept going, they ultimately would have succeeded, but logic flees when emotion kicks in. For this reason, it is important for the sake of momentum to protect our emotions. The best way to protect emotions is with urgency.

Now You Know

An emotional commitment to success must be made and continually cultivated to reach the top at whatever you do.

With undisciplined emotions as the reason many don't make it the sales industry, understand that disciplined emotional decisions are the reason people make it to the top of their companies. Put another way, the emotional reasons we tie to our goals and dreams are generally what keep us focused on the tasks that need to be completed to see our goals to the end. In my career, I've seen many talented people fail to make it because of a lack of emotional stability or a lack of emotional ties to their dreams. In essence, John Maxwell's book entitled *Talent Is Never Enough* is an appropriate statement for these individuals. The other side of the coin is that I've seen plenty of non-talented individuals who have had a burning desire and a strong *why* persevere and eventually develop the skills laid out in this book, enabling them to reach the top of their field.

An emotional commitment to success must be made and continually cultivated to reach the top at whatever you do. For this reason, urgency can affect your emotions. Let's now look at how urgency affects our beliefs, which in turn affect our actions, which in turn affect our results. We will do this by using the example of the pipeline again.

The Urgency Effect #2: The Pipeline and The Urgency Effect #3: Your Posture

When I teach about momentum and urgency, I almost always bring up the pipeline. Although we touched on this in a previous chapter, the following concept, taught with a different approach, will emphasize how filling the pipeline with urgency can ensure momentum.

Often, the only thing you need to do to create momentum is to fill your pipeline with urgency. As I said in the previous chapter, conducting ten presentations over a ten-week period (one per week) yields a completely different result than ten presentations completed in a ten-day period. This understanding of filling the pipeline with urgency also has its benefits in posture. Somehow, when the pipeline is full, your posture is strengthened. When urgency is thrown in the mix, you get a lethal dose of momentum.

When people first learn about the previous six laws, it's easy for them to fall into the trap of thinking they might not know as much as they thought they did. If this is you,

I have some great news to share: when it comes to sales, *urgency overcomes skill*!

Let me illustrate why by showing how a full pipeline and the right posture can be transformed when mixed with urgency.

If you are conducting one presentation per week, you are more inclined to feel like you need that sale. This message translates to your prospects and affects how they receive you. If they tell you no, which according to Law #6, will happen more often than not, you will have had everything riding on that outcome for that week. This creates an emotional devastation that affects your belief, which affects your actions and then your results. In the end, there is no momentum, and you may start to think your product or company doesn't work.

On the other hand, if you conduct one presentation per day, or five per week, then let's look at what happens: During your presentation on Monday, you know in the back of your mind that you have four additional presentations taking place that week. This creates a sense of security that transfers to your prospect. The message being sent to your prospect is that you don't need him for anything. Furthermore, you can *genuinely feel* you don't need him because you have four backup presentations coming right up. If you keep the pipeline full, then you can always have this posture. This translate into a growing belief, which motivates more consistent action and ends with a much higher closing ratio (better results) based on Law #5.

The fact is that urgency affects everything. It affects your posture, your productivity with appointments, and your ability to close the sale. It also affects any momentum you desire to create. It ultimately affects your attitude, goals, lifestyle, and retirement. It has an impact on all other areas of your life.

The Urgency Effect #4: Your Prospect List

Many people fail to understand the difference between true urgency and being pushy. There is a huge difference. Remember that true urgency—the speed at which you pursue your goals and dreams—will not annoy other people. If you are operating under true posture, you will be working consciously with Laws #1, #2, and #3. Therefore, if someone isn't ready to move at your pace, you simply take it away, move on, and add that prospect to a later list. Urgency should be a systematic approach. Again, it boils down to keeping the pipeline full and operating with complete urgency.

In just about every form of sales, you have a prospect list. People often work their lists improperly, without any system of urgency. Within this is mind, I teach a two-list approach. Notice how urgency is tied to this system, and apply it to yours.

The two lists I work are my Active Prospect List and my 30/60/90-Day List (also known as my Later List). My Active Prospect List falls under the mentality that urgency is the primary determining factor of whether or not a prospect can stay on this list. This system also helps me psychologically overcome challenges that typically occur when things don't happen as fast as I want them to. It also helps provide clear direction on how I should be spending my time. This mostly translates into continually figuring out more ways to fill the pipeline.

Now You Know

Urgency affects everything. It affects your posture, your productivity with appointments, and your ability to close the sale.

Here's how it works. Let's say you start with a list of twenty prospects. You place their names on your Active Prospect List. Once they are added to this list, you have twenty-four to forty-eight hours to find out whether they qualify to look at what you have. You can do this with nothing more than a simple prequalification call. You'll find that if you leave names on your active list for longer than twenty-four to forty-eight hours, you are more likely to continue to postpone the phone call because of overthinking what the prospect might say or do. In addition, make it your goal to have ten or more active prospects on your list at all times to ensure that your pipeline remains full. If, when prequalifying a prospect, his or her timing doesn't seem right for an appointment, you can always ask this question before hanging up, "Do you mind if I call you in about sixty days to check in and let you know how I'm doing?"

This question can be asked even the prospect says he or she isn't interested. You will discover that your prospect will almost always answer yes. At that point, decide whether he or she is worthy of a call back. Remember, you are the one interviewing the prospect. And again, it relates back to posture. If your prospects are worthy, you can move them to your Later List and remove them from your visual range. If you leave prospects you've called and who aren't interested on your Active Prospect List, it gives you the false impression that you have more going on than what you really do. Those prospects' names actually become distractions, and this sets you up for emotional disaster.

If an active prospect continues through to the point of the presentation, you can then start a twenty-four to forty-eight hour time frame in which you expect to close the sale. Why twenty-four to forty-eight hours? It has been proven that if the sale doesn't close within twenty-four to forty-eight hours, there is a high probability that it never will. I set myself up to believe that if the close doesn't happen with urgency, it won't happen at all. In addition, if after twenty-four to forty-eight hours, I can sense that a sale isn't going to happen, I shift to the takeaway and move the prospect to my Later List.

Now You Know

The urgency mindset can duplicate throughout your entire organization. Unfortunately, a lack of urgency can also duplicate.

When I first began to make significant money in sales, I discussed this very topic with other top producers within the industry, and I discovered that they felt the same way as I did about the twenty-four to forty-eight hour time frame. Furthermore, I have found that those who keep prospects on their active lists for longer than this period of time experience a major reduction in momentum because they spend most of their time chasing down prospects. They also trick themselves into thinking they have a lot more going on than they really do. This, in turn, messes up their pipeline and their emotional state of mind, resulting in almost no momentum.

Again, urgency is everything. Of course, there are exceptions for prospects who have legitimate short-term delays. In addition, follow up with the sharp prospects on your Later List, and discard the not-so-sharp ones in the trash can. I encourage you to do this because I have known many no's that thirty (or more) days later converted into high profits. The important thing is that you transfer these prospects back into your Active Prospect List and remain focused on that list to keep your pipeline full. This two-list system has proved to be simple, yet extremely effective, in my quest to create the mindset of urgency.

The Urgency Affect #5: The Urgent Team (Duplication)

When applied correctly, the urgency mindset I described will duplicate throughout your team and your entire organization. Unfortunately, a lack of urgency can also duplicate. I have found that organizations that have momentum usually began with one person who sustained an urgent mindset and backed it up with action for a certain period of time. This soon transferred to other team members, and before they knew it, there was a mighty force to reckon with.

As your team grows, you can literally create a culture for urgency. When building teams of salespeople, you have a window of opportunity in which to create the proper expectations of high performance. When new salespeople join your team—whether they are hired or working as an independent representative—proper engagement with urgency is crucial. In fact, how you get your new team members started could be the single biggest factor contributing to team momentum that you ever duplicate. Because it is difficult to change bad habits, it is extremely important to carefully craft the ways in which you get a new salesperson started.

People do what they see and not what they hear, just like the old saying—"What you do is so loud that I can't hear what you say." This means urgency is taught primarily through your actions and not through what you try to get others to do.

Remembering that urgency is the speed at which you pursue your goals and dreams, let's conclude with an idea about how fast you can create it for your life. Generally, urgency can be started in any thirty-day period. This also means there is a thirty-day period that will become a defining time for the rest of your success. The interesting thing about this thirty-day period is that you get to pick when it is. I'm talking about a thirty-day period full of massive action and urgency, a thirty-day period that will continually reinforce the right belief, which will encourage the right action, which will allow the right results to take place. Understand that the actions needed to succeed within your system, when applied with urgency, allow you to overcome most of the learning curve in your skill. It generally takes about ninety days to see the beginnings of major momentum, so do give it some time. Don't expect to have a thriving organization or to become the top salesperson overnight. In many cases, it may even take a year or two to be able to witness massive momentum. The reality, however, is that once it does happen, you'll be able to look back and point to a period of time when the activity began that ultimately led you to the momentum you're experiencing. And in all cases, it started with a decision followed by a thirty-day period.

By creating a habit and achieving your desired results, that thirty-day run will lead to ninety and so on until you reach your ultimate destination. You cannot reach that destination without setting out on your journey, and that journey is best started with thirty days of urgent activity. It is my wish for you that there are no more delays in progress, and that the next thirty days of your endeavor will be full of the right actions, because the right activity always equals the right results.

Now You Know
You have everything it takes to perform at a much higher level than you ever thought possible. You just have to tap into it.

You're Sitting on Oil

Let me end with a final story. Perhaps you've heard about an elderly gentleman who lived back around the mid-1900s. He owned a nice big piece of property in the state of Texas. He was filing bankruptcy during the Great Depression. The man owned a piece of land that had been inherited and passed down to him through several generations. He had lived on this land his whole life. During the Depression, he had lost nearly everything. One day some businessmen approached him and said, "Sir, we would like to dig on your property. We think there might be oil underneath your land." Initially, the man said no, because he thought the drilling might decrease the value of his property, but after speaking to his wife, they decided there was nothing to lose. "We're going to lose this piece of property anyway," they reasoned. The couple agreed to let the oil company come in and start the process. Within a few days, the oil company struck what turned out to be the largest oil well in this country's history. Instantaneously, the elderly man went from being poor to being a multimillionaire. Or did he? In actuality, he had owned this land his entire life. Was he now just becoming a millionaire, or had he been a millionaire his entire life and just not known all he had to do was to tap into what was already there?

You have everything it takes to perform at a much higher level than you ever thought possible. You have been sitting on oil way too long. You just have to tap into it. So, focus on your *why* and get busy, because urgency affects everything!

Now You Know how urgency can affect your emotions and how your level of urgency could be the single most important area of development you ever master. Urgency affects your pipeline, your posture, and the momentum of your entire team. *Now You Know* the monumentally important Law of Urgency, which tells you that the speed at which you pursue your goals affects everything!

 # AFTERWORD

IN THE BEGINNING OF this book, I presented the question, "Why do some succeed, and others fail when using the same system?" These seven laws have revealed the answer to that question. To end this book, I would like to leave you with one final thought: Action is the best teacher! Many seem to make the mistake of wanting to learn everything prior to massive amounts of action. Every top producer I've worked with, however, created a massive amount of activity, thus accelerating his or her learning. You have an advantage. If you begin to apply these seven laws and initiate a massive action plan, your rate of success will accelerate beyond your imagination. With this in mind, I encourage you to determine the speed at which you want to reach your goals and dreams. Take action today!

For additional **Now You Know** *resources, visit me at* **www.ryanchamberlin.com.**

ABOUT THE AUTHOR

Since his early twenties, Ryan Chamberlin has been fortunate enough to work with and train some of the top salespeople in the United States. When he began his sales career, Ryan sold various products and services with very little success. This soon changed when he began applying the information contained within the pages of this book. Eventually, these principles helped Ryan develop one of the largest organizations in the direct sales industry. Although he struggled early on, Ryan earned his first million while still in his twenties by implementing the Now You Know methodology. He has since been asked to oversee multiple companies training divisions and serve on various corporate advisory councils. Ryan co-pioneers systems using the theories behind what he calls, "the seven laws of sales." At the date of this writing, these systems continue to produce hundreds of millions of dollars in revenue for several companies.

Today, Ryan is one of the most sought after speakers and motivators in the industry. He spends the majority of his time consulting and coaching many top salespeople and leaders on how to leverage themselves, and maximize their team-building efforts. Now You Know, his first book, reveals the seven laws he has taught to thousands, and the exact system that he utilized to accelerate his success. These laws are timeless sales principles that can be applied to any sales industry by people who are looking to reach their highest possible potential.

Ryan is also co-author of the books *The Mentor – A Network Marketing Story* with Frank Viscuso, and *The Rich You Formula* with best selling author and speaker Gary Smalley.

Ryan lives in Belleview, Florida with his wife Jenny and four boys—Alexander, Andrew, Anthony, and Avery. For more information, including free sales tips and resources, or to contact Ryan, visit Ryanchamberlin.com.